How the
Best
Leaders
Lead

How the Best Leaders Lead

Proven Secrets to Getting the Most Out of Yourself and Others

Brian Tracy

AMACOM

American Management Association

New York • Atlanta • Brussels • Chicago • Mexico City • San Francisco
Shanghai • Tokyo • Toronto • Washington, D.C.

This publication is designed to provide accurate and authoritative
information in regard to the subject matter covered. It is sold with
the understanding that the publisher is not engaged in rendering
legal, accounting, or other professional service. If legal advice or other
expert assistance is required, the services of a competent professional
person should be sought.

Library of Congress Cataloging-in-Publication Data

Tracy, Brian.
   How the best leaders lead : proven secrets to getting the most out of yourself
and others / Brian Tracy.
      p.   cm.
   Includes index.
   ISBN-13: 978-0-8144-1434-7
   ISBN-10: 0-8144-1434-6
   1. Leadership.   2. Management.   I. Title.

HD57.7.T724   2010
658.4'092—dc22

                                                                 2009044946

About AMA
American Management Association (www.amanet.org) is a world leader in talent
development, advancing the skills of individuals to drive business success. Our mission
is to support the goals of individuals and organizations through a complete range of
products and services, including classroom and virtual seminars, webcasts, webinars,
podcasts, conferences, corporate and government solutions, business books and
research. AMA's approach to improving performance combines experiential
learning—learning through doing—with opportunities for ongoing professional growth
at every step of one's career journey.

Printing number

10   9   8   7   6   5   4   3   2   1

This book is fondly dedicated to Roger Joseph, my friend and business partner for many years and one of the most competent and inspirational leaders I have ever met.

Contents

CONTENTS

The Race Is On

"Great hopes make everything possible."
—BENJAMIN FRANKLIN

We are living in the most challenging times for business and economics that we have experienced in our lifetimes. Only the fit will survive. The race is on, and you are in it. If you are not committed to winning, to conquering against all odds, you will be brushed aside and passed over by people and companies more determined to win than you are.

Some time ago, Harvard University made three predictions that apply to the current economic situation. First, they said, there will be more change in your business in the year ahead than ever before. Second, there will be more competition in your business than ever before. And third, there will be more opportunities in your business than ever before.

But these opportunities will be different from the business that you are accustomed to in the present, and you must move quickly to take advantage of them if you are going to survive and thrive against your competitors.

As it happens, these predictions were made in 1952. A fourth prediction was added later: Those individuals and organizations that do not quickly adapt to the inevitable and unavoidable changes of today will be in different fields or out of business within one or two years.

Charles Darwin said, "Survival goes not necessarily to the strongest but to the species that is most adaptable to changing circumstances."

Damon Runyon once wrote, "The race is not necessarily to the swift, nor the contest to the strong, but that's the way to bet."

You have heard the old saying that the Chinese character for *crisis* is the same character used for *opportunity*. This is because within almost every crisis there is an opportunity of some kind, if you can find it.

Brilliant on the Basics

When Vince Lombardi took over the Green Bay Packers, he was asked if he was going to change the players, the plays, the training, or other key aspects of the team. He replied, "I'm not going to change anything; we are simply going to become brilliant on the basics."

The Green Bay Packers had been doing poorly for some years. In his first meeting with the team, he famously picked up a football and said, "Gentleman, *this* is a football."

From then on, Lombardi concentrated on the basics, running drills aimed at making his team faster and more effective at executing plays than any other team. He took the Green Bay Packers to two Super Bowl Championships and made football coaching history.

Consistent with the Lombardi method, the key to leading and succeeding in times of crisis and rapid change is to become "brilliant on the basics."

In this book, based on my work with more than a thousand companies in fifty-two countries, I will share some of the best thinking and action skills used by top executives and company owners to achieve outstanding results in difficult markets against determined competition.

When you practice these ideas and put them into action, you will get results out of all proportion to your efforts. Sometimes a single change in direction, inspired by an insight or an idea in this book, can change your business, and your life, quickly and dramatically.

The Seven Responsibilities of Leadership

There are seven basics that never change, the key responsibilities of leadership in any organization. On a scale of 1 to 10, your ability in each of these seven areas determines your value to yourself and your contribution to your organization. Here they are:

Your First Responsibility: Set and Achieve Business Goals

The number-one reason for business and executive failure is the inability to achieve the sales, growth, and profitability goals for which the leader is responsible.

Setting and achieving business goals embraces every part of strategic and market planning, including products, services, people, productivity, promotion, finances, and competitive responses. We will touch on these critical factors in the pages ahead.

The Second Responsibility of Leadership: Innovate and Market

As Peter Drucker said, the purpose of a business is to "create and keep a customer."

Only through continuous innovation of products, services, processes, and promotional methods can companies create and keep customers. As Bruce Henderson of the Boston Consulting Group wrote, "All strategic planning is market planning."

The Third Responsibility of Leadership: Solve Problems and Make Decisions

Ds are unported

This is so important that I will dedicate an entire chapter to the problem solving and decision making skills that you absolutely must master to be an effective leader. Remember, a goal unachieved is merely a problem unsolved. A sales target unachieved is a problem unsolved. The only obstacles that stand between you and the business success you desire are problems, difficulties, hindrances, and barriers. Your ability to go over, under, or around these problems is central to your success.

The Fourth Responsibility of Leadership: Set Priorities and Focus on Key Tasks

One of the most important jobs you do is to deploy limited resources, especially of people and money, into those areas where they can make the greatest contribution to the success of the enterprise.

The law of the excluded alternative says, "Doing one thing means not doing something else."

Time is your scarcest resource. It is limited, perishable, irretrievable, and irreplaceable. The way you allocate your time can be the critical determinant of everything you achieve—or fail to achieve.

The Fifth Responsibility of Leadership: Be a Role Model to Others

Albert Schweitzer once wrote, "You must teach men at the school of example, for they will learn at no other."

Throughout the ages, the example that you establish in your character, attitude, personality, and work habits, and especially the way you treat other people, sets the tone for your department or organization.

You do not raise morale in an organization; it always filters down from the top. There are no bad soldiers under a good general.

One of the great questions for you to continually ask yourself is, "What kind of a company would my company be if everyone in it was just like me?"

Marshall Goldsmith, top executive coach for senior executives in the Fortune 1000, has demonstrated over the years that a single change in a behavioral characteristic of a key executive can cause a positive multiplier effect that impacts the behavior of an enormous number of people.

Leaders conduct themselves as though everyone is watching, even when no one is watching.

The Sixth Responsibility of Leadership: Persuade, Inspire, and Motivate Others to Follow You

Tom Peters said that the best leaders don't create followers, they create leaders. It's true that you want your people to have initiative and the liberty to act on that initiative. But all initiatives must be in the support and service of what you are trying to achieve as a leader.

If people aren't following you, you are not a leader. If no one is listening to you, believes you, or cares what you say, you are not going to succeed. If people are only going through the motions to earn a paycheck, the greatest business strategy in the world will fail.

You must motivate others to follow your vision, to support and achieve the goals and objectives that you have set, to buy into the mission of the organization as you see it. Today, getting others to follow you takes more than command and control. You have to earn their trust, respect, and confidence. That is the key to sustainable success as a leader.

The Seventh Responsibility of Leadership: Perform and Get Results

In the final analysis, your ability to get the results that are expected of you is the critical factor that determines your success.

In the pages ahead, I will show you a series of simple, proven, practical methods and techniques used by top executives and business owners everywhere to get better, faster, and more predictable results in any business or organization or in any economic situation.

Each Crisis Contains an Opportunity

"Professional soldiers pray for peace, but hope for war."

What does this saying mean? It means that soldiers pray for peace because war is so terrible: Every sensible person wants to live out their life in peace and for as long as possible, including soldiers.

But only during warfare, during critical moments on the battlefield, is it possible to achieve distinction and be rapidly promoted. Professional soldiers hope for war, in the back of their minds, so they can demonstrate their fitness and capability for higher command.

Viktor Frankl, a survivor of Auschwitz during World War II and the founder of Logotherapy, famously wrote, "The last great freedom is the freedom to choose your own mental attitude under any set of conditions."

A senior executive friend of mine, whose company had suffered sales declines of 40 percent in less than a year and was reeling from the reversals in the economy, told me how he maintained a positive attitude every day.

He said, "Each morning, when I get up, I have a decision to make. I can be happy, or I can be *very* happy. I therefore decide that today, I will be very happy, and I allow that attitude to guide me throughout the day, no matter what happens."

You too can choose your own attitude under any given set of circumstances. You can decide to be positive, constructive, and forward-looking. You can look upon each "crisis" as an "opportunity," even if it is only an opportunity for you to grow, mature, become stronger, and perhaps even achieve the kind of "battlefield promotions" that will stay with you for the rest of your career.

Welcome to the twenty-first century!

& what are the chosen choice

CHAPTER ONE

The Heart of a Leader

"Character may be manifested in the great moments, but it is made in the small ones."

—WINSTON CHURCHILL

Leadership is the single most important factor in the success or failure of a company or business. Your ability to step forward and lead your enterprise to success in competitive markets is both essential and irreplaceable.

The better you become as a leader, the better you will be in every area of your enterprise. Fortunately, leaders are made, not born. As Peter Drucker wrote, "There may be such a thing as a natural born leader, but there are so few of them, that they make no difference in the great scheme of things."

Leaders are primarily self-made, self-developed. They work on themselves continually, learning, growing, and becoming more capable and competent over the years.

Leaders usually emerge to deal with a situation that requires leadership skills. A manager can work successfully at fulfilling his responsibilities and getting the job done for many years. Then a crisis occurs, and leadership is required. At that time, the leader steps forth and takes charge of the situation. He or she becomes a different person and fulfills a different role.

Follow the Rules

General Norman Schwarzkopf tells about his first experience of leadership at the Pentagon. His senior officer told him that to do his job well, all he had to do was to "Follow rule 13."

When he asked, "What is rule 13?" his commanding general said, "When placed in command, take charge!"

When then Colonel Schwarzkopf asked, "But after I have taken charge, how do I make decisions?"

His commanding officer said, "Simple. Use rule 14."

When Colonel Schwarzkopf asked, "What is rule 14?" he was told, "Do the right thing!"

These are excellent ideas for you, as well. When placed in command, take charge, and if ever you are in doubt about what to do, simply do the right thing.

Leadership Requires Character

Leadership is more about who you are than what you do. Your ability to develop the qualities of effective leadership, the essence of what it takes to be a leader, is more important to your success as an executive than any other factor.

One of the great principles of personal development is, "Whatever you dwell upon grows and expands in your experience and personality."

You become more effective, day by day, when you think and act on the basis of the key qualities of effective leaders throughout the ages. You program these qualities into your personality and behavior by dwelling on them continually. You learn these qualities by practicing them in your daily activities as a person and as a leader in your organization.

The more of a leader you become in the *inside*, the more effective you will become in all your leadership activities on the *outside*. You become more of a leader by thinking the same way that top leaders think.

The Seven Qualities of Leadership

There have been more than three thousand studies conducted over the years aimed at identifying the qualities of successful leaders, especially successful military leaders who have won important battles against great odds in turbulent theaters of warfare—which very much describes succeeding in the marketplaces of today.

More than 50 qualities have been identified that are important to leadership. But there are seven qualities that seem to stand out as being more important than the others. The good news is that each of these qualities can be learned, and they must be learned by practice and repetition.

1. Vision: The Most Important Single Quality of Leadership

Leaders have vision. They can see into the future. They have a clear, exciting idea of where they are going and what they are trying to accomplish. This quality separates them from managers. Having a clear vision turns the individual into a special type of person.

This quality of vision changes a "transactional manager" into a "transformational leader." While a manager gets the job done, a true leader taps into the emotions of his people.

In times of rapid change and turbulence, it's a good idea to occasionally call a "time out." Stop the clock. Back off. Take some time to think about who you really are inside, what you stand for, where you are going, and what kind of a future you want to create for yourself and your organization.

In their book, *Competing for the Future*, Gary Hamel and V.K. Prahalad emphasize the key role of "future intent" to business success. They explain that the greater clarity you have with regard to the future you wish to create, the easier it is for you to make the day-to-day decisions necessary to reach that future.

As a leader, in order to remain calm and centered in times of rapid change, you must continually ask two questions: "What are we trying to do?" and "How are we trying to do it?"

You must play your own game rather than allow yourself to be knocked off center by unexpected setbacks and difficulties. You achieve this by developing a clear vision for yourself and your organization and then by sharing this vision of an ideal future with the people who look up to you and depend upon you for leadership.

Developing Your Vision

Begin with your values. What are the organizing principles of your business that you believe in and stand for? What are the core values and beliefs that animate and motivate you? What are the values that your company practices and incorporates into all of its activities?

The difference between leaders and average people is that leaders have clear beliefs that they will not compromise under any circumstances. Average people have fuzzy or unclear values that they will compromise for short-term advantage.

Based on your values, imagine the perfect future for your business.

Imagine that you have all the time and money, all the knowledge and experience, all the people and resources—everything you need. What does your business look like?

Once you are clear about your values and your ideal future, draw up the mission statement for your company—what your company is trying to accomplish. Be specific. "Our mission is to offer the highest quality products and, as a result, grow at a rate of 20 percent per year in sales and profitability" is better than "Our mission is to offer exciting products in a spirit of innovation and entrepreneurship."

Beyond the specific mission, you should know the core purpose of your company—why it exists. What kind of contribution does your company make to enhance the well-being of your customers?

Your company's purpose is very important. It is your real reason for being in business. Your belief in the goodness of your purpose is what enables you to persevere against external problems and difficulties. It is what motivates and inspires your people to put in the extra effort and go the extra mile.

As Nietzsche said, "A man can bear any *what* if he has a big enough *why.*"

The "why" is the emotional component of leadership and is always defined in terms of how you and your organization serve and contribute to the lives and well-being of your customers. It is what your products or services actually do to improve their lives and work.

Finally, leaders are goal-oriented. Set specific, measurable, time-bounded targets that you must hit and numbers that you must achieve in order to get from where you are to wherever you want to go in the future with your organization.

In every case, clarity is essential.

Perhaps the most important contribution you make to your organization in times of rapid change in competitive markets is to help everyone to remain calm, clear, focused, and forward-thinking concerning your values, vision, mission, purpose, and goals. This is the starting point of great leadership.

2. Courage: The Second Quality That Leaders Have in Common

"Courage is rightly considered the foremost of the virtues, for upon it, all others depend." (Winston Churchill)

General Douglas McArthur once wrote, "There is no security in life; only opportunity."

The quality of courage means that you are willing to take risks in the achievement of your goals with no assurance of success. Because there is no certainty in life or business, every commitment you make and every action you take entails a risk of some kind. This is why courage is the most identifiable outward quality of a great leader.

The fact is that the future belongs to the risk-takers, not the security-seekers. The future belongs to leaders who are willing to move out of their comfort zones and take the necessary risks that are required for the enterprise to survive and thrive in any economic situation.

Boldness means the willingness to initiate action with no guarantees. Samuel Johnson wrote, "Nothing will ever be attempted if all possible objections must first be overcome."

The more information you gather and opinions you seek before you make an important decision, the more likely it will be that the decision will be the right one. But you can never eliminate the element of risk. It always exists.

Audacity Is the Key to Victory

Frederick the Great, who was renowned for his propensity to attack the enemy no matter what the odds, said, "L'audace! L'audace! Y toujours l'audace!'' (Audacity! Audacity! And always audacity!)

Robert Green, in his book *The Laws of Power,* said, "Always be audacious. Audacity will get you into trouble occasionally, but even more audacity will usually get you out."

The practice of boldness and audacity means that you continue to think in terms of actions you can take. You practice what is called the "continuous offensive." You dare to go forward in all circumstances.

By continually taking aggressive action in the direction of your goals, you put yourself on the side of the angels. The more action-oriented you become, the greater will be your confidence and the more likely it will be that you will do the right things at the right time that lead to victory.

Hang in There

An essential part of courage is called "courageous patience": the ability to stay the course and not give up when you do not seem to be making any progress, or when things are going against you.

After every great offensive action begins, there is a period when things slow down, and often nothing seems to be happening, neither victory nor defeat. In this gap, many people lose heart and retreat or withdraw, or, even worse, fight on half-heartedly.

But the leader, once committed to a course of action, continues to persevere, carry through, and push forward with the same vigor and energy with which he began.

In 1941, in the darkest days of World War II, Winston Churchill's cabinet members were urging him to "make peace" with Hitler. Churchill absolutely refused to consider the idea. He gave his famous speech, which ended with those stirring words, "We will never surrender!"

When he was asked privately why it was that he was so ada-mant about fighting on in the face of overwhelming odds, he re-plied, "Because I study history. And history tells you that, if you hold on long enough, something always happens."

This conversation took place in November 1941. On December 7, 1941, the Japanese bombed Pearl Harbor. Two weeks later, Hitler declared war on the United States, bringing the United States and its great industrial power into the war on the side of England, changing the course of history.

The Ultimate Challenge

The ultimate test of courage in leadership is how well you per-form in a crisis. The only thing that is inevitable and unavoidable in the life of the leader is crisis. This is the testing time.

Your ability to function well in a crisis largely determines the success or failure of your organization. This ability cannot be taught in a classroom. It is only developed when you actually face a real crisis—a real emergency with serious potential losses.

One of the qualities that I have observed over the years is that, when presented with a crisis, an unexpected reversal, or a setback, leaders immediately become calm. They take a deep breath and deliberately slow down. They have learned over time that the calmer you remain in a crisis, the better you can think, analyze, and decide.

The crisis is the true testing time of leadership. During the crisis, you demonstrate to yourself, and everyone who is watch-ing you, what you are really made of, deep inside.

The key to dealing with a crisis effectively is to decide, in ad-vance, that no matter what happens, you will remain calm, cool, and relaxed. You resolve in advance that you will not become angry or upset. You will get the information you need, make the decisions that are required, and take the actions that are necessary. This is the true mark of leadership.

3. Integrity: The Most Respected and Admired Quality of Superior People and Leaders in Every Area of Activity

In every strategic planning session that I have conducted for large and small corporations, the first value that all the gathered executives agree upon for their company is integrity. They all agree on the importance of complete honesty in everything they do, both internally and externally.

Some years ago, after all the executives around the table had agreed that integrity was the most important of all values in the company, the president, one of the richest men in America, made a statement that I never forgot. He said, "It seems to me that integrity isn't really a value in itself; it is simply the value that guarantees all the other values."

In his bestselling book *Winners Never Cheat,* Jon Huntsman, who started a chemical company from scratch and grew it into a $12 billion enterprise, writes, "There are no moral shortcuts in the game of business—or life. There are, basically, three kinds of people: the unsuccessful, the temporarily successful, and those who become and remain successful. The difference is character."

The core of integrity is truthfulness. Integrity requires that you always tell the truth, to all people, in every situation. Truthfulness is the foundation quality of the trust that is necessary for the success of any business.

Steven Covey says that the key to earning the trust of others is to be "trustworthy." Imagine that everything that you do or say is going to be published in the local newspaper. Always tell the truth, no matter what the price, because the price of not telling the truth is going to be even higher. Jack Welch says the lack of truthfulness, or "candor" in his words, can destroy any business. "Lack of candor basically blocks smart ideas, fast action, and good people contributing all the stuff they've got. It's a killer."

A key part of trustworthiness is to always keep your promises. You should give promises carefully, even reluctantly, but once you have given a promise, you must always follow through on that promise.

The natural extension of personal integrity is quality work. A person who is truly honest with himself continually strives to do excellent quality work in the service of his customers.

It seems that the very best companies, those that are famous for the quality of their products and services, also have the highest internal ethical standards.

The Reality Principle

When he was the president of General Electric, Jack Welch was interviewed in *Fortune Magazine* and asked what he considered to be the most important principles of leadership. He said that the most important principle, in his estimation, was what he called the Reality Principle.

Welch defined this principle as, "Seeing the world as it really is, not as you wish it would be."

He was famous for going into a problem solving meeting and immediately asking, "What's the reality?"

The Reality Principle is a practical application of the value of integrity. It requires truthfulness and honesty. It requires dealing in a straightforward way with the reality of the situation, based on facts rather than hopes, wishes, or assumptions.

Accepting Responsibility

Leaders with integrity are responsible. They accept responsibility for themselves and for getting the results that they have been hired and appointed to achieve. Leaders continually remind themselves, "I am responsible."

Leaders say, "If it's to be, it's up to me."

Leaders refuse to make excuses when things go wrong. Instead, they make progress. They refuse to dwell on what might have happened; instead they focus on what can be done now to resolve the problem.

Leaders do not blame other people for mistakes. The leader accepts that "the buck stops here."

4. Humility: Leaders Have the Security and Self-Confidence to Recognize the Value of Others

The best leaders are those who are strong and decisive but also humble. Humility doesn't mean that you're weak or unsure of yourself. It means that you have the self-confidence and self-awareness to recognize the value of others without feeling threatened. It means that you are willing to admit you could be wrong, that you recognize you may not have all the answers. And it means that you give credit where credit is due. Jim Collins writes that the best leaders "Look in the window, not the mirror, to apportion credit for the success of the company."

Humility gets results. Larry Bossidy, the former CEO of Honeywell and author of the book *Execution*, explained why humility makes you a more effective leader: "The more you can contain your ego, the more realistic you are about your problems. You learn how to listen, and admit that you don't know all the answers. You exhibit the attitude that you can learn from anyone at any time. Your pride doesn't get in the way of gathering the information you need to achieve the best results. It doesn't keep you from sharing the credit that needs to be shared. Humility allows you to acknowledge your mistakes."

Bossidy learned the difference between humility and weakness from his mother, who told him, "It's not a question of thinking less of yourself; it's a question of thinking of yourself less."

Forget your ego, and focus instead on what's right for the company. Don't let an overblown opinion of yourself get in the way of finding the right answers and the right solutions to problems. Don't be afraid to recognize and use the strengths of others. Jack Welch said he always wanted to be surrounded by people smarter than he was.

Don't believe that humility will undermine your authority in the eyes of others. The opposite is true. Reckless arrogance does not inspire confidence; self-assured humility does.

As former New York City mayor Rudy Giuliani writes in his book *Leadership*, "Leaders of all kinds—CEOs, coaches, even the occasional mayor—run the risk of thinking they are where they are because of divine intervention. When selected for a position of leadership, do not believe you were selected by God. That's exactly when humility should be applied. What are my weaknesses? How can I balance them?"

Continuous Learning

The hallmark of humble leaders is that they continually strive to get better. They never stop learning. They don't believe that they know everything there is to know, that they have nothing more to learn. As Pat Riley, the basketball coach, said, "If you're not getting better, you're getting worse."

Charlie Jones, the businessman and speaker, often said, "You will be the same person in five years that you are today except for the people you meet and the books you read."

Learn from the people you meet and work with. Listen as much as you talk.

And as with any student, don't be afraid to hit the books.

Zig Ziglar said, "Not all readers are leaders; but all leaders are readers."

Reading is to the mind as exercise is to the body. Resolve today to read 30 to 60 minutes daily in your field. This amount of reading will translate into one book per week, 50 books per annum, and 500 books in 10 years. When you read regularly to upgrade your knowledge and skills in your field, you soon develop the winning edge that gives you an advantage over people who are less informed.

5. Foresight: Leaders Have the Ability to Look Into the Future and Anticipate What Might Occur

Excellent leaders are good strategic thinkers. They have the ability to look ahead, to anticipate with some accuracy where the industry and the markets are going.

Leaders have the ability to anticipate trends, well in advance of their competitors. They continually ask, "Based on what is happening today, where is the market going? Where is it likely to be in three months, six months, one year, and two years?"

Because of increasing competitiveness, only the leaders and organizations that can accurately anticipate future markets can possibly survive. Only leaders with foresight can gain the "first mover advantage."

Leaders are astute in what I call *extrapolatory thinking*. They have the ability to accurately predict what is likely to happen in the future based on what is happening in the present. They accurately predict the consequences of their actions and the consequences of the changes taking place in the current market.

Project Forward

The extrapolatory thinking and foresight of leaders cover all aspects of the business. What is it that your customers want, need, and are willing to pay for today? Based on current trends, what kinds of products and services will they be demanding in the future? Based on your current results, what changes are you going to have to make to ensure that your products and services of tomorrow are exactly what the customers will be wanting at that time?

A key aspect of foresight is crisis anticipation. Leaders look down the road into the future and ask, "What could possibly happen that could threaten the survival of my business?"

Leaders think clearly about the future. They think about what might happen. They think about what they are trying to accomplish today and what might happen to interfere with their plans for tomorrow.

Only leaders can think about the future. This is one of their primary jobs. No one else in the organization is tasked with this degree of future orientation. The greater accuracy with which leaders can predict the likely consequences of their actions and the changes in the market, the greater the success of the business will be.

What are the worst possible things that could happen to your business in the months and years ahead? Of all those things, what would most threaten the survival of your business? And what could you do, starting today, to make sure that the worst possible events do not occur?

The more information you gather and the more people you talk to, the greater your clarity about future conditions will be. The greater clarity you have, the better your decisions will be for taking actions to guard against the possible crises or to take advantage of the possible opportunities.

One of the best tools to help leaders anticipate both crises and opportunities is called *scenario planning*. A wide variety of problems, setbacks, and unpleasant surprises can befall your company in the long term. Scenario planning gets you thinking about what could go wrong so you prepare for the future today. With scenario planning, you develop three or four detailed scenarios of your company and its environment 5, 10, or 20 years down the road (the number of years depends on how quickly change can dramatically affect your industry). Each scenario is filled with details; you describe not only your product line, customers, and competitors, but all the other environmental factors that could impact your business, such as new federal regulations. Once you have filled in the scenarios, you can then take realistic, short-term steps to prepare for the scenarios. Does one scenario anticipate a new competitor underselling you with cheaper products? If so, what do you need to do today to reduce costs and increase the value of your product?

With scenario planning, you can identify the worst possible things that might happen that could affect the ability of the company to survive. Then, make a plan to ensure that if one of those reversals took place, you have already developed a strategy to deal with it.

6. Focus: The Ability to Focus Personal and Corporate Energies and Resources in the Most Important Areas Is Essential to Leadership

Leaders always focus on the needs of the company and the situation. Leaders focus on results, on what must be achieved by themselves, by others, and by the company. Leaders focus on strengths, in themselves and in others. They focus on the strengths of the organization, on the things that the company does best in satisfying demanding customers in a competitive marketplace.

Your ability as a leader to call the shots and make sure that everyone is focused and concentrated on the most valuable use of their time is essential to the excellent performance of the enterprise.

The natural human tendency, at home and at work, is toward entropy, toward a dissipation of energy, toward diffusion of effort and "majoring in minors."

As Goethe said, "The things that matter most must never be at the mercy of the things that matter least."

The job of the leader is to help every person in the company achieve laser-like focus on the most valuable contributions they can make to the growth of the enterprise. And, of course, the leader must lead by example. The leader must be a role model. If you want everyone else to concentrate on their highest value activities, you must do the same, every hour of every day.

How do you recognize the highest value activities? The answer lies in your core competencies and the core competencies of your organization.

Start with your *personal* core competencies; what is it that you do extremely well? What special skills and abilities have been most responsible for your personal success to date? What is it that you, and only you, can do, that, if done well, will make a real difference to your organization?

What are the core competencies of your *organization*? What is it that your company does especially well? What makes your company superior to your competition? What are the areas where you are recognized as a leader in your industry? What should those areas be in the future?

What are your most profitable and successful products and services? Who are your best and most productive people? What are your most important markets, and who are your most valuable customers?

Focus on the Future

Leaders are intensely solution-oriented, not blame-oriented. They think in terms of solutions most of the time. They think about what can be done immediately to resolve the situation, rather than who did what and who might be to blame for the problem in the first place.

Leaders focus on the future, on the opportunities and actions of tomorrow, rather than the problems and difficulties of yesterday.

Leaders do not complain or criticize. They remain positive and focused on their goals and the goals of the organization.

One of the keys to calmness and mental clarity is to refuse to spend a single second worrying or becoming angry about something that you cannot change. And in most cases, you cannot change a past event. If something has happened, like spilled milk, there is nothing you can do about it.

Instead, focus your precious mental and emotional energies on what can be done, and on what others can do, to deal constructively with the situation now and solve the problem today.

The only real antidote for worry is purposeful forward action. As the leader, you should get so busy working on the solution, on the future, that you have no time to think about what happened in the past and how it might have been avoided.

7. Cooperation: The Ability to Work Well with Others Is Essential for Effective Leadership

Your ability to get everyone working and pulling together is essential to your success. We will talk about the key elements of building an effective team later in this book. Just remember that leadership is the ability to get people to work for you because they want to.

The 80/20 rule applies here. Twenty percent of your people contribute 80 percent of your results. Your ability to select these people and then to work well with them on a daily basis is essential to the smooth functioning of the organization.

Gain the cooperation of others by making a commitment to

get along well with each key person every single day. You always have a choice when it comes to a task: You can do it yourself, or you can get someone else to do it for you. Which is it going to be?

You Become What You Think About

The greatest principle ever discovered, which underlies all religion, psychology, and philosophy, is, "You become what you think about most of the time."

Most of the time, leaders think about the qualities of leadership and how to apply them daily.

Leaders have a clear vision of where they are going, and they convey this vision to everyone around them.

Leaders have the courage to take risks, to move forward, to face danger with no guarantee of success.

Leaders have integrity. They deal honestly and straightforwardly with each person. They tell the truth, and they always keep their word.

Leaders are humble. They get results by using the strengths and knowledge of those around them. They know how to listen, and they know how to learn.

Leaders have foresight. They continually look ahead and anticipate what might happen. They make provisions to guard against possible reversals and put themselves into a position to take advantage of possible opportunities.

Leaders focus on what's important. They concentrate their time and resources, and the time and resources of the company, on the activities that will make the most difference.

Leaders cooperate well with others. They are liked and respected by everyone around them. They go out of their way to get along well with the key people upon which the company depends. They truly believe that people are their most valuable asset.

The best companies have the best leaders. The second-best companies have the second-best leaders. The third-best companies, in these times of turbulence, are unfortunately on their way out of business.

The most important contribution you can make to your company is to be a leader, accept responsibility for results, and dare to go forward.

CHAPTER TWO

Leaders Know Themselves

"You will either step forward into growth, or you will step backward into safety."

—ABRAHAM MASLOW

The better you know and understand yourself, the better decisions you will make and the better results you will get.

What is the most important and valuable work that you do? The answer is *thinking*. The quality of your thinking determines the quality of your choices and decisions. The quality of your decisions, in turn, determines the quality of your actions. The quality of your actions determines the quality of your results, and the quality of your results determines almost everything that happens to you, especially in business.

One of the most important words in thinking and action is *consequences*. An action is important if it has serious potential consequences. An action is unimportant if it has few or no potential consequences.

Your thinking, and the actions you take based on that thinking, can have enormous consequences. Your decision to introduce a new product or service, hire or fire a key person, or make an investment in a particular area can all have significant consequences.

Perhaps the most powerful stimulant of good thinking is pointed questions that force you to analyze and decide exactly what you want and what you are going to do to achieve it. The questions that follow will not only help you focus on your goals and aspirations; they will help you to develop greater clarity about who you really are inside and what is truly important to you.

These questions are both personal and professional. The successful leader is first and foremost a successful person. The best leaders establish priorities and goals not only for their professional lives but for their personal lives as well. They know in both their professional and personal lives what they want, who they are, who and what is important, where they are going and why, and what strengths and weaknesses will help or hinder them as they move forward. The best leaders are complete, balanced, self-aware, healthy individuals who live their professional and personal lives by the same rules.

Pay special attention to all of these questions. If your answers to any of these questions are wrong—if you have the wrong priorities, for example, or lack the self-awareness to know your true strengths and weaknesses, or pick the wrong skills to develop—this alone can cause you to make the wrong choices and decisions and sabotage your ability to get the results that are expected of you.

Answer the following questions:

1. What is your current *position*?

_____

2. What are the *three* most important things you do in your work?

    1. _____

    2. _____

    3. _____

3. How do you *measure* results, success, and accomplishment in your work?

    1. _____

    2. _____

    3. _____

4. What are your *special* abilities and talents?

    1. _____

    2. _____

    3. _____

5. What tasks do you *perform* especially well?

    1. _____

    2. _____

    3. _____

6. What are your three most important *goals* in your work?

    1. _____

2. _____

3. _____

What specific *actions* could you take immediately to achieve these goals?

1. _____

2. _____

3. _____

7. What are your three most important goals in your *family* and *personal* life?

   1. _____

   2. _____

   3. _____

What specific *actions* could you take immediately to achieve these goals?

1. _____

2. _____

3. _____

8. What are your three most important *financial* goals?

   1. _____

   2. _____

   3. _____

What specific *actions* could you take immediately to achieve these goals?

1. _____
2. _____
3. _____

9. What are your three most important *health* goals?

1. _____
2. _____
3. _____

What specific *actions* could you take immediately to achieve these goals?

1. _____
2. _____
3. _____

10. What are your three most important *career* goals?

1. _____
2. _____
3. _____

What specific *actions* could you take immediately to achieve these goals?

1. _____
2. _____
3. _____

11. What three *skills* could you develop that would help you the most to achieve your most important goals?

    1. _____

    2. _____

    3. _____

What specific *actions* could you take immediately to achieve these goals?

    1. _____

    2. _____

    3. _____

12. What are the three greatest *opportunities* in your life, right now?

    1. _____

    2. _____

    3. _____

What could you do immediately to *take advantage* of these opportunities?

    1. _____

    2. _____

    3. _____

13. What are your three biggest *worries* or *concerns* in life, right now?

    1. _____

2. _____

3. _____

What steps could you take immediately to *resolve* these worries or concerns?

  1. _____

  2. _____

  3. _____

14. What three *personal* qualities do you have that you are most proud of?

  1. _____

  2. _____

  3. _____

15. What three *weaknesses* do you have that you would like to overcome?

  1. _____

  2. _____

  3. _____

16. What *three words* would you like people to use to describe you when you pass away?

  1. _____

  2. _____

  3. _____

17. What are your three most important *business values?*

    1. _____

    2. _____

    3. _____

18. What are the three most important *values* that guide your *relationships* with your family and others?

    1. _____

    2. _____

    3. _____

19. Who are the *most important people* in your work?

Name	**Position**
1. _____	_____
2. _____	_____
3. _____	_____
4. _____	_____
5. _____	_____
6. _____	_____
7. _____	_____

20. Who are the most important people in *your personal life?*

Name	**Relationship**
1. _____	_____
2. _____	_____

3. _____   _____

4. _____   _____

5. _____   _____

6. _____   _____

7. _____   _____

21. What are your favorite *non-work* activities?

    1. _____

    2. _____

    3. _____

22. What would you do if you were forced to *take a day off*?

    1. _____

    2. _____

    3. _____

23. What would you do if you were forced to *take a month off* and you had an unlimited budget?

    1. _____

    2. _____

    3. _____

24. What would you do with your life if you learned today that you only had *six months to live?*

    1. _____

2. _____

3. _____

25. What would you do if you had *$20,000,000* in the bank but only *10 years to live?*

    1. _____

    2. _____

    3. _____

    4. _____

    5. _____

26. What goals would you set for yourself if you were *guaranteed* complete success?

    1. _____

    2. _____

    3. _____

27. What *three activities* in life or work give you your greatest feelings of happiness and self-esteem?

    1. _____

    2. _____

    3. _____

28. What three activities or tasks do you enjoy *the least?*

    1. _____

2. _____

3. _____

29. If you could only do three things all day long at work, what *three activities* contribute the greatest value to your company?

    1. _____

    2. _____

    3. _____

30. If you could wave a magic wand and *make your life perfect* in every respect, what would each area look like?

    a. Business, career, income?

        1. _____

        2. _____

        3. _____

    b. Family, relationships, lifestyle?

        1. _____

        2. _____

        3. _____

    c. Finances, savings, investments?

        1. _____

        2. _____

        3. _____

d. Health, weight, fitness?

    1. _____

    2. _____

    3. _____

e. Personal life and activities?

    1. _____

    2. _____

    3. _____

There are only four ways to change your life: First, you can do *more* of certain things. Second, you can do *less* of other things. Third, you can *start* doing something that you have not done before. Fourth, you can *stop* doing certain things altogether.

31. What activities in your life or work should you be doing *more of?*

    1. _____

    2. _____

    3. _____

32. What activities in your life or work should you be doing *less of?*

    1. _____

    2. _____

    3. _____

33. What are the new activities in your life or work that you should *start* doing?

     1. _____
     2. _____
     3. _____

34. What are the activities in your life that you should *stop* doing altogether?

     1. _____
     2. _____
     3. _____

35. Knowing what you now know, is there any situation in your life or work that you would *not get into today* if you had to do it over?

     1. Work? _____
     2. Staff? _____
     3. Investments? _____
     4. Health?
     5. Family? _____
     6. People? _____
     7. Activities? _____
     8. Other? _____

36. List *10 goals* in your life that you would like to accomplish in the future, based on your answers to the above questions:

Start each goal with "I." Write in the present, positive tense, as though it were already a reality. Attach a deadline to it.

For example, you could write, "I earn $XXX,XXX by December 31, 200__." or "I weigh XXX pounds by June 30, 200__."

1. _____

2. _____

3. _____

4. _____

5. _____

6. _____

7. _____

8. _____

9. _____

10. _____

37. Imagine that you could wave a magic wand and have any one of the above goals *within 24 hours.* Which *one* goal, if you achieved it, would have the greatest positive impact on your life?

_____

_____

38. Write your answer to question #37 in the present tense, a positive, personal statement starting with

the word "I," exactly as if your goal has already been achieved:

_____

_____

39. Set a deadline on this goal; exactly when do you want to achieve it?

_____

40. Identify the main obstacles you will have to overcome to achieve this goal:

    1. _____

    2. _____

    3. _____

41. Identify the additional knowledge, information, or skills you will have to acquire to achieve this goal:

    1. _____

    2. _____

    3. _____

42. Make a list of the people whose help and cooperation you will need to achieve this goal. (Be sure to include your family.)

    1. _____

    2. _____

    3. _____

43. Make a list of the things you will have to do—the steps you will have to take—to achieve this goal:

   1. _____

   2. _____

   3. _____

   4. _____

   5. _____

   6. _____

   7. _____

44. From the steps above, what one action are you going to take immediately to achieve your most important goal?

   _____

   _____

Leaders know themselves. They know who they are and what they want. The greater clarity with which you can answer these questions, the more effective you will be as a leader.

You will make better decisions, set clearer priorities, allocate people and money more intelligently, and efficiently utilize your personal time and resources to accomplish more of those things that are more important. You will make fewer mistakes and get more things done with greater effectiveness.

By developing complete clarity about yourself and your situation, you will think and act more efficiently and accomplish greater results in everything you do.

CHAPTER THREE

Counterattack! Business Lessons from Military Strategy

*"You can do anything you wish to do, have anything
you wish to have, be anything you wish to be."*
—RICHARD COLLIER

Your ability to lead your company to market success, to achieve
victory against enormous odds, is the key measure of your success as a leader. Every skill and ability that you can bring to bear
to help increase sales and profitability gives you an added advantage that enables you to perform at your best.

Great generals and military leaders have been studied
throughout history to determine which qualities and abilities en-
abled them to prevail against fiercely determined and hostile
enemy forces. Over the years, students of military history have
identified 12 principles of military strategy that, when properly
applied, lead to victory.

In every case, when one or more of these principles was ignored or not implemented properly in a battle, it led to defeat
and, in some cases, to the loss of a war or the collapse of an
empire.

These principles of military strategy apply to business, as well. Every one of them is essential to success in competitive markets. A weakness in a single key area can lead to business reversals, or even bankruptcy. We see this around us and in the financial press on an almost daily basis.

Military Principles of Strategy

In my book *Victory,* I expanded on each of the principles of military strategy and demonstrated how they can be applied to business, sales, and personal life. In this chapter, I will give you a brief overview of each principle and how you can apply it to be a more effective leader and lead your organization to victory as well. Here they are:

1. The Principle of the Objective

This refers to the importance of establishing clear objectives for every military action in advance and making them clear to each person who is expected to help to achieve those objectives.

As with military leaders, business leaders must establish clear objectives for every business action. Objectives are the short- and medium-term sub-goals that will eventually lead to your overall goal for the company.

All strategy, however, begins with deciding exactly what is to be accomplished in the long term. Clarity is essential. What exactly are your goals for the company or organization that you are leading?

Leaders must not only set the organization's goals but also effectively communicate those goals to those they lead. Does everyone in your company know exactly which goals you are trying to achieve in your business, in what order of priority, by what date, and how they are to be measured?

Four Questions to Ask

When you are setting goals and objectives, there are four key questions that you must continually ask when you are setting objectives:

1. *What are you trying to do?* What are your goals in terms of sales, growth, cost reductions, cash flow, and profitability? What are they based on? Are they realistic?

2. *How are you trying to do it?* What specific methods and techniques are you using to achieve these goals? Are they working? Could there be a better way?

3. *What are your assumptions?* Assumptions can be both explicit and clearly stated or implicit and simply accepted without question. They are fixed ideas that you believe are true; the basis for your decisions and actions.

4. *What if your most cherished assumptions were wrong?* For example, there are some basic assumptions common to every business: there is a genuine market need for what you are selling, and you can produce and sell the required product or service in sufficient quantities and at a high enough price to make a profit. What if these assumptions were no longer true? What changes would you have to make in your business?

While leaders need to be decisive and confident, one of the most valuable qualities you can develop as a leader is openness to the possibility that you could be wrong. In times of rapid change, you might be a little bit wrong, a lot wrong, or completely wrong. This doesn't mean that you are, but your willingness to consider that you *could* be wrong opens your mind to new thinking and new ideas. Sometimes assumptions are based on the past, not the present. The answers to these questions about your objectives and the new realities of your situation shift continually, especially in fast-changing markets. You must be prepared to change as well.

As Alec Mackenzie once wrote, "Errant assumptions lie at the root of every failure."

The GOSPA Method

There is a simple formula for strategic thinking that you can use to dramatically sharpen your ability to set and achieve the goals and objectives that are essential to the success of your organization. It is called the GOSPA Method.

The acronym GOSPA stands for: Goals, Objectives, Strategies, Plans, and Activities.

Set Clear Business Goals

Your goals are the specific, measureable, long-term results that you want to achieve one, two, three, and five years in the future. Business goals must be clear, written, and specific. They must be measureable and exact. Your goals must be time-bounded, with deadlines and sub-deadlines.

Long-term goals can be both qualitative and quantitative. A qualitative goal may be, "We are recognized as offering the highest quality product or service in our market by at least one national publication."

A quantitative goal is one that can be expressed in numbers

and financial terms. Some examples of quantitative goals include:

1. The levels of sales volume that you want the company to attain within a year, two years, or whatever timeframe you decide

2. Gross profit margins on sales

3. Net profit margins on sales

4. Return on equity invested in your business

5. Your stock price at certain points in the future

Imagine a ladder leaning against a building. The top of the ladder represents your goals: where you want to end up at the end of a particular business period. As Steven Covey says, "Before you start scrambling up the ladder of success, make sure it is leaning against the right building."

Be Clear About Your Objectives

Your objectives are the sub-goals that you must accomplish to achieve the larger goals. In using the analogy of a ladder leaning against a building, your objectives are the rungs on the ladder, the steps that you will have to take to achieve your ultimate financial goals.

If you want to double your company's gross profit margins within two years, what steps can you take over the next two years to achieve that goal? If within the next five years, you want your stock price to recover the value it lost over the past five years, what steps can you take now and in the short- and mid-term to achieve that goal?

Different goals will demand different objectives. It is your role as leader to determine the appropriate objectives to achieve the goals you established in the first step. For example, recovering your market value may require selling off underperforming business units. Increasing margins may require eliminating low-margin product lines.

Your success or failure in business will be largely determined by your ability to accurately determine your objectives and then to follow through in an excellent fashion to achieve each of these objectives on time and to a necessary level of quality.

Determine Your Strategies

Strategies are the specific ways that you accomplish each of the objectives that you set in the previous step. There are a variety of different methods and techniques that you can use. The strategy that you choose can be the critical factor in your success or failure. You must select your strategies with care.

For each objective, develop several alternate strategies. Always have a Plan B. You are only as free as your well-developed options. Never allow yourself to get stuck with only one course of action.

For example, there are more than 20 different ways to sell a product and more than 20 different ways to get the money you need. Most companies limit themselves to one or two of these instead of continually exploring alternatives. Keep expanding your thinking by asking, "How else can we achieve this objective?"

Evaluate each of your options based on the true capabilities of your organization. One of the biggest flaws in business thinking is, "Because I want to, I can." In many cases, you can have a clear idea of what you should or could do but lack the financial capability or internal competencies to achieve it. Sometimes the lack of one critical person in a key position makes it impossible for you to achieve a particular objective.

In developing your strategies, consider the situation in the marketplace. Who are your customers, and what do they want? Who is your competition, and how are they likely to respond to your strategy to take business away from them?

In developing strategies to achieve your critical objectives, always have a clear idea of what you will do if your initial plan is not successful. The rule is to "Assume the best and plan for the worst." Ask, "What is the worst thing that can happen if we launch this strategy and it is unsuccessful? What will we do then? What would our fallback position be?"

Make Detailed Plans for Accomplishment

Your plans are the steps that you and your organization will take to implement your strategies in each area. Create a plan by listing everything that your company will have to do to achieve a particular objective within a particular strategy.

The 20/80 rule says, "The first 20 percent of time that you spend planning to achieve your goals and objectives will save you 80 percent of the time in execution."

Prior to the invasion of Europe, the officers of the Allied Command worked for almost two years on planning and preparing for the D-Day invasion. After the invasion, during which innumerable things failed to happen as expected, General Eisenhower was asked about the value of the plan. He replied, "The plan was nothing, but the planning was everything."

The purpose of planning, the principle of the objective, is to force you to think through every critical element and step that will be necessary to achieve the goal before you make irrevocable commitments and take irretrievable actions.

In your planning, start by listing all the resources that you will need to achieve your objectives, especially the money and people required.

Make sure that you have the capabilities to carry out this strategy within your organization, or that you have these capabilities available to you through outsourcing or other companies.

Once your list of steps is complete, organize your activities by priority and sequence.

To organize your activities *by priority*, determine what is more important and what is less important. Of all the things that you could do to carry out your strategy and to achieve your objective, what is the most important action you could take?

Organize activities *by sequence* by determining what you will have to do first, what you will have to do second, and in what order the other tasks will have to be done.

In planning your strategy, think in terms of parallel activities as well as sequential activities. Parallel activities are activities that can be done at the same time. Sequential activities are activities that require that something be done before something else is done.

All excellent executives and leaders are good planners. They take the time to think, plan, and decide before they take action. There is a rule that says, "Every minute spent in planning saves ten minutes in execution." The more time you take to think before you act, the more effective you will be, the better the results you will get, and the greater predictability you will have regarding those results.

Action Is Everything

Activities are the individual tasks that have to be completed by everyone in the organization—from the leadership team at the top to the employees on the front lines—in order for you to implement the plan, apply the strategy, achieve the objective, and accomplish the goal. All the greatest strategic thinking in the world and all the greatest planning is useless if you do not convert that thinking and planning into action. The GOSPA Method leads you from general long-term goals to specific short-term plans. The final step in the method is simply to do.

Once you know where you want to go and how you want to get there, you must decide upon a specific day-to-day plan of action and then launch strongly. In military terms, this is the *attack*. Leaders always think in terms of the specific actions they can take, and they resolve to take them quickly and decisively.

Manage the Plan

Once you have gone through the GOSPA Method, you can manage by objectives. You can set clear work goals for yourself and others and then ensure that everyone achieves those goals.

Whatever those goals might be, the same rules of clarity and communication apply. As the leader, you must ensure that all the components of GOSPA are clearly understood throughout the organization. Neither the goals, objectives, strategies, plans, nor action can be achieved by you alone, the entire organization must participate.

To manage by objectives, take the time to explain, discuss, and get people to agree upon their individual objectives before you begin. Make each assignment measurable and time-bounded.

Manage by responsibility: Make people responsible for results. Put them in charge. Delegate both the job and the responsibility for getting it done. Set deadlines for completion of each task. When a person knows that she is responsible and that you are counting on her, she will often perform the task at a higher level than you might have expected.

Managing by objectives is not only about communication

and delegation. It also means that leaders provide the required support to their organization. Communicate your objectives, then provide the financial, personnel, or any other kind of support needed to achieve those objectives. The best leaders are not only great communicators and delegators, they are also great enablers.

2. The Principle of the Offensive

This refers to switching over to the attack, to taking aggressive action against the enemy to achieve victory.

Napoleon said, "No great battles are ever won on the defensive." Your company cannot win by playing it safe, by retreating, or by simply cutting costs.

To succeed on any competitive battlefield, you must seize the initiative. You must always be attacking, moving forward, continually innovating and marketing in new and better ways.

The most important number in any business is cash flow. The purpose of business warfare is to generate sales, revenues, and cash flow in a steady, predictable, consistent process in the face of determined competitors who also want the same thing.

In business, the equivalent of the offensive, or the attack, in warfare is marketing and sales to your customers.

The key to business success is increased sales activity and sales results. Success requires advertising, promoting, marketing to, and attracting prospective customers and then selling effectively and converting them into buyers. In times of economic uncertainty, every effort and activity in the organization must be focused on sales generation and new customer development.

The primary reason for business success is high sales; the primary reason for business failure is low sales. All else is commentary.

The Key Question for Business Success

In a military situation, the military unit—whether it's a platoon, a battalion, or an entire Allied military force—will succeed by shooting their guns, firing their artillery, launching their missiles, grenades, and torpedoes, and dropping their bombs. These actions, however, are not done in a haphazard, freewheeling manner. A military offensive is a concerted, organized effort, with a role for every component, from the general to the private. It works because the unit's leaders asked and answered a series of questions—questions such as what or whom is to be attacked, why is it being attacked, and with what personnel and matériel will it be attacked.

While military leaders have little problem keeping all the members of the unit focused on how to achieve victory—defeat the enemy with military force—business leaders have to work harder to keep the business organization focused on its path to victory. As I said above, the only path to business victory is to sell more.

I have developed a summary series of questions that you can ask and answer regularly to ensure that your company, and everyone in it, is focused on acquiring customers and selling more.

"**What** exactly is to be sold; **to whom** is it to be sold; **why** will the customer prefer our product or service to that of our competitors; **how** are customers to be identified and attracted; **how** are they to be sold and **by whom**; **how much** are we going to charge; **how** are we going to charge this amount; **how** is the product going to be paid for; **how** will our product or service be produced and delivered; **how** will it be serviced and maintained; and **how** will all of these activities be monitored and managed?

Let us look at each of these questions individually:

63

1. What exactly is to be sold?

2. To whom is it to be sold?

3. Why will the customer prefer our product or service to that of our competitors?

4. How are customers to be identified and attracted?

5. How are they to be sold?

6. By whom are they going to be sold?

7. How much are we going to charge?

8. How are we going to charge this amount?

9. How is the product going to be paid for?

10. How will the product be produced and delivered?

11. How will it be serviced and maintained?

12. How will all of these activities be monitored and managed?

We will deal in greater detail with the answers to these questions in chapter four. In the meantime, how clear are you and the key people in your company about the answers to each of the above questions? As a leader, your job is not only to know the answers, but to make sure everyone in the organization knows the answers—every answer. A wrong answer to any of these questions can lead to serious consequences and even failure of the business. Make sure that everyone knows his or her role as it relates to the answer to each question. Employees not only need to know what products your company sells, for example; they need to know what the product choice (or product price range or customer service plan) means to their function in the organization. Think of the military offensive: Soldiers not only know the target to be attacked, they know how that target choice translates into action for them.

3. The Principle of the Mass

This principle refers to the ability of the commander to concentrate his forces at one point, the location of the enemy's greatest vulnerability.

In business, your ability to focus your company's limited resources and energies on its greatest potential opportunities is the key to personal and corporate success. If you consider your biggest competitor the enemy, to use the military term, then seek out those areas in which it is most vulnerable. A competitor may be trying to expand its product lines into areas where your company has a longer history and greater name recognition. Focus your efforts and resources on defeating the competitor in those areas.

The principle of the mass is not only about weakening the opposition; it is also about strengthening your own company. One of your greatest responsibilities as a leader is to identify and monitor the critical success factors of your business. What are the most important numbers or metrics that best indicate the health of your business and the success of your activities? Look not only for the obvious numbers, such as market share or return on investment, but also the less obvious, such as the ratio of international versus domestic revenue. Have your international sales been increasing steadily over the past five years, while domestic sales have stayed flat? If so, you may have greater opportunity for international growth than you realized, while the domestic market may be saturated.

With this new information, you may want to dedicate more resources and more time to international marketing activities and fewer resources and time (at least less than in the past) on domestic activities.

The 80/20 rule, also known as the Pareto principle, is a powerful exercise to help you focus on areas where you have the greatest opportunities for growth and success. Italian economist Vilfredo Pareto first developed the 80/20 rule when measuring the distribution of wealth in Italy in the early 1900s. He found that 80 percent of the wealth was held by 20 percent of the people. It was American quality pioneer Joseph Juran, however, who really discovered the power of the 80/20 rule when he realized that it applied to all areas in business.

Apply the 80/20 rule to every aspect of your own company.

1. Who are the 20 percent of customers who account for 80 percent of your business?

2. Which are the 20 percent of your products and services that account for 80 percent of your sales volume?

3. What are the 20 percent of your sales and marketing activities that account for 80 percent of your sales?

4. What are the 20 percent of your sales and marketing methods that attract 80 percent of your new customers?

5. What are the 20 percent of your products, services, and business activities that account for 80 percent of your profits?

Each answer reveals where you should be focusing the forces at your command: your company's people, money, and competencies. For example, your customer retention initiatives should be targeted to the 20 percent of customers who account for 80 percent of your revenues. They are the ones you want to keep.

Your ability to concentrate single-mindedly on those activities that represent the greatest potential value to your business is an essential quality of leadership, indispensable to success.

4. The Principle of Maneuver

This principle refers to the ability to move the attacking forces in such a way that they can outflank the enemy and attack where the enemy is most vulnerable.

Almost all great military victories are the result of speed and movement. The principle of maneuver applied to business refers to innovation and flexibility.

With innovation, you continually seek faster, better, cheaper, easier, and more effective ways to produce and sell your products and services. One small improvement over your competitors can give you an edge in the marketplace.

Flexibility means that you continually try new things, in new ways. You refuse to get stuck in a comfort zone or fall in love with your current method of doing business.

Apply Zero-Based Thinking in Every Area

Perhaps the most powerful single tool that you can use to remain flexible and effective in times of rapid change is what I call *zero-based thinking*.

With zero-based thinking, which comes from zero-based accounting, you continually ask, "Knowing what I now know, is there anything that I am doing today that I would not start up again today, if I had to do it over?"

I call this a Knowing What I Now Know (KWINK) analysis. You conducted a personal KWINK analysis in chapter two (see question 35). Now it's time to analyze your business. In times of rapid change, you will continually find that ideas and plans of action that seemed reasonable or even excellent at the time are no longer relevant and may even be counterproductive.

Make a habit of applying zero-based thinking to every part of your business:

1. Is there anyone working for you, anyone you have hired, assigned, or promoted, who, knowing what you now know, you would not hire, promote, or assign?

    1. _____

    2. _____

    3. _____

2. Are there any products or services that, knowing what you now know, you would not develop or bring to the market again today?

    1. _____

    2. _____

    3. _____

3. Are there any services that you offer to your customer in conjunction with your other business activities that you would not start up again today, knowing what you now know?

    1. _____

    2. _____

    3. _____

4. Are there any business expenditures, in any area, that, knowing what you now know, you would not authorize again today?

    1. _____

    2. _____

    3. _____

5. Are there any business processes or activities in your business that, knowing what you now know, you wouldn't start up again today, if you had to do it over?

    1. _____

    2. _____

    3. _____

6. Are there any investments or commitments of time, money, or emotion that, knowing what you now know, you wouldn't get into again today?

    1. _____

    2. _____

    3. _____

How can you tell if you are in a situation where zero-based thinking needs to be applied? It's simple: stress! Whenever you experience chronic stress, or ongoing irritation or dissatisfaction begins to follow you around, ask yourself, "If I was not doing this, would I get into it again today?"

Face the Reality

Whenever you reach the point where you have identified a zero-based thinking situation, if your answer is "No, I would not get into this situation again if I had it to do over," your next question is, "How do I get out of this situation, and how fast?"

The primary reason that people get stuck in zero-based thinking situations is because of ego. They cannot admit that they made a mistake. They are afraid to tell others that they have changed their mind. They don't want to face up to the fact that they were wrong in their original decision.

But this is not for you. Do a KWINK analysis on every part of your life where you are experiencing stress or aggravation of any kind.

It takes tremendous courage to admit that you are not perfect, that you have made a mistake, and that one of your cherished decisions from the past has turned out to be wrong. But as soon as you admit that a zero-based thinking situation has occurred and you then move to eliminate it, all your stress will disappear.

Over the years, I've worked with thousands of executives in the area of zero-based thinking. After they have finally admitted that they wouldn't get into that situation again, knowing what they now know, and they moved to resolve it as quickly as possible, they all had the same reaction: "I should have done this a long time ago."

Once you decide to bite the bullet and deal straightforwardly with a situation that is not working out, you will experience a great sense of freedom and exhilaration. All your stress will disappear. All of your mental energy will then be available to you to focus on the future, to focus on what you can do and accomplish rather than worrying about a bad situation.

5. The Principle of Intelligence

The principle of intelligence refers to the need to obtain excellent information concerning the actions and movements of the enemy.

In military terms, the more that the commander knows about the opposition forces, their numbers and deployments, the better able he is to plan the strategy necessary to defeat them.

In business, the more you know and understand about your competitors and your marketplace, the more successful you will be. The more time you take to thoroughly understand your marketplace, your main competitors, and their most attractive product offerings, the more insights you will gain, which will enable you to take the actions necessary to make sales in a tough market.

Working closely with your leadership team, create a competitive analysis grid comparing yourself and your products or services to each of your main competitors.

1. What are their major products and services? Who do they sell them to? Why do those customers buy from our competitors rather than from us?

2. What is our competitor's reputation? What do people say about our competitor that causes them to appear to our potential customers as a more desirable supplier of our product or service?

3. What is the perceived quality of their product or service? On a scale of one to ten, what is their quality ranking in the marketplace in comparison to us? Customers always buy what they perceive to be the very best quality possible for the amount

they are prepared to spend. How do we compare with our competitors in this area?

4. What are our competitors' prices for products and services similar to what we offer? Are our prices higher or lower than theirs? Could we change the competitive structure of our market by altering our prices in some way?

5. What kind of people do our competitors have as executives, managers, and staff? How do our people compare with theirs? Are they aggressive about training and upgrading their people? Do they pay more to attract better people? How can we position our company against them with regard to human resources?

6. What is the quality of their sales force? Do they have excellent salespeople who are thoroughly trained and professionally managed? The company with the best salespeople always sells more than the company with lesser quality salespeople.

7. What is their competitive advantage? What is their area of excellence? In what way are our competitors perceived to be superior to us, and what could we do to offset that?

In some companies, leaders do not know the answers to these important questions—not because they don't ask the questions, but because they are not being told the right answers. The principle of intelligence, in business and in the military, depends on the flow of good intelligence from the front lines to the commanders. You alone cannot develop the information needed to answer these questions. Yet there are many reasons why your people could withold the right answers from you. Do you punish bad news? Do you play the blame game? Do you refuse to believe any information that you don't want to hear? If you react negatively or destructively to bad news, you will not get the answers you need to make the right decisions.

Once you have a realistic and honest appraisal of the competition, based on honest, unconstrained information, continually ask yourself, "How can we use our brains and abilities to outmaneuver our competition?" Anyone can spend more money, but innovative marketing takes creativity.

6. The Principle of Concerted Action

This refers to the ability of the general in command to ensure that all parts of his forces work together in harmony and cooperation in both offensive and defensive operations.

A well-organized, smoothly functioning, highly professional modern army can defeat a disorganized army several times its size. We see this in modern warfare, where small armies, well commanded and coordinated, achieve great victories against overwhelming odds. We have seen this in Middle Eastern conflicts going back as far as the victory of Alexander the Great over Darius at the Battle of Arabella, in 323 BC, when Darius's million-man army was defeated by 50,000 crack Macedonian troops under Alexander.

The equivalent in modern business is the team. All work is done by teams. All top companies have excellent, efficient, well-ordered teams that function effectively to achieve business results.

Today, the manager's work is the work of the team. The manager's job is to organize and facilitate the team so that it achieves excellent results. Choosing the members of your team is so important that we will examine it in greater depth in chapter five. We will discuss the art of team building in detail in chapter eight.

7. The Principle of Unity of Command

This refers to the need for absolute clarity about who is in charge of every area of activity, from the commanding officer on down.

Top companies have clear leadership at all levels. Everyone knows who is in charge.

For an individual to function effectively, he or she must only have one boss and be required to report to only one person.

As the leader, you must be absolutely clear about your performance expectations for each person. Everyone must know exactly what you want them to do, by when, and to what standard of quality.

Perhaps one of the best ways to achieve and maintain unity of command is for you to hold regular meetings and discussions with your staff, complete with agendas and follow-up assignments. The best leaders and the best organizations meet often to share information and discuss the work.

8. The Principle of Simplicity

This principle refers to the importance of clear, simple orders, commands, and battle plans that are easily understood by the people expected to carry them out.

A good plan is easily understood and easily executed. Good leaders strive for simplicity in every request and discussion.

One of the keys to ensuring simplicity and understanding is to think on paper. Make sure that people take notes and write things down during discussions.

The greater the number of steps in any work process, the greater the likelihood of misunderstandings, mistakes, additional costs, and delays in completion. The very act of eliminating steps and minimizing complexity dramatically increases both efficiency and effectiveness in business operations.

9. The Principle of Security

This principle refers to the importance of guarding against surprise attacks or unexpected reversals.

In business, the most important job of the leader is to ensure the survival of the enterprise. The principle of security requires that you look down the road and anticipate what could happen to hurt your business or to threaten its survival.

One of the keys to the survival of a business is so simple that it is sometimes overlooked or taken for granted: cash. Cash is not the same as sales revenues or profits. An automobile dealer who sells a $40,000 car has made $40,000 in sales revenue. But he doesn't have any cash from that sale until the institution that is financing the sale pays the dealer.

Cash is king. To ensure that your business survives and thrives, you should receive from your accounting staff clear, conservative cash projections for the next six to twelve months. You should carefully monitor and manage cash flow on a weekly, even daily, basis. You should do everything possible to build financial reserves and provide against unexpected setbacks or financial shortfalls.

Running out of cash is just one of the surprises or unexpected reversals that can threaten a company. How do you prepare for other surprises, such as a new competitor attacking your market share, a new product that makes your current products obsolete, changes in customer preferences, new government regulations that impact your business, or any of the other potential surprises that might be waiting around the bend? The core of a business is simple: You make money when customers buy your products;

more customers mean more money and a greater chance of long-term survival for your business. The core of a business is simple, but the threats and surprises that can sink your company can come from a wide variety of sources.

One of the best tools to help leaders ensure the long-term security of their companies is called *scenario planning*. There is a wide variety of problems, setbacks, and unpleasant surprises that can befall your company in the long term. Scenario planning gets you thinking about what could go wrong so you can prepare for the future today. With scenario planning, you develop three or four detailed scenarios of your company and its environment 5, 10, or 20 years down the road (the number of years depends on how quickly change can dramatically affect your industry). Fill each scenario with details; describe not only your product line, customers, and competitors, but also all the other environmental factors that could impact your business, such as new federal regulations. Once you have filled in the scenarios, you can then take realistic, short-term steps to prepare for them. Does one scenario anticipate a new competitor underselling you with cheaper products? If so, what do you need to do today to reduce costs and increase the value of your product?

With scenario planning, you can identify the worst possible things that could happen that could affect the company's ability to survive. Then make a plan to ensure that if one of those reversals takes place, you have already developed a strategy to deal with it.

Scenario planning is a leadership activity, but, once again, your decisions and actions are only as good as the information you receive. Make sure that scenario planning sessions include employees and managers from all levels of the organization; the scenarios you develop must be based on reality—and reality is not necessarily the view from the top.

10. The Principle of Surprise

This principle refers to the importance of taking an action that is not anticipated by the enemy.

All great victories are the result of surprise, of doing something completely different from what the enemy expected.

In your market, conducting business the same old way is probably not going to work. You must be looking for different ways to do business with different customers, in different markets, at different prices, using different distribution channels.

In the military, they use a strategy called a *force multiplier*. This is a factor that an attacking force can use to increase its hitting power, even though it has fewer troops and armaments.

One of the most powerful force multipliers is speed. The Blitzkrieg used by the Germans in World War II is a good example. General George Patton used the force multiplier of speed to race across Europe in the latter part of World War II, encircling German armies and capturing thousands of towns and troops at a speed seldom seen in the history of warfare.

When you have a good idea in your business, implementing that idea with speed can give you an advantage over your competitors.

You can also use creativity, the ability to find faster, better, cheaper ways to deliver your product or service, as a force multiplier.

Focus and concentration are force multipliers as well. Your ability to concentrate your energies on key customers and markets can give you hitting power far in excess of your actual size or resources.

You can use the principle of surprise by doing exactly the opposite of what you have been doing up to now. For example, instead of selling your product, your company offers to give it away. But in order for the customer to get the "free" product, he or she has to sign an expensive service contract to ensure that the product continues to operate properly.

Be prepared to abandon one market altogether and concentrate your resources in a different market. Intel transformed itself and the high-tech world by abandoning the low-cost, low-margin chip market and going full blast into the micro-processor market. The rest is history.

Continually seek new ways of generating profits from your existing resources. How could you combine your products or services to create new, more valuable offerings? How could you break your products or services into smaller component parts to make them more attractive or affordable to your current customers?

The greatest enemy of using the principle of surprise in business is the Not Invented Here syndrome (NIH). To counter this tendency, you should continue looking at different businesses in different markets, offering your products and services to different customers and seeking ways to approach your market in unexpected ways.

Be aware that many leaders sabotage the principle of surprise in their own companies. Creativity and innovation require flexibility and risk. Your managers and employees aren't going to try something new if they are not allowed to fail. Your managers and employees aren't going to try combining products into higher value offerings or breaking products into smaller components if they are punished when their initiative fails to live up to expectations. Nor will your managers and employees try something new if they are not given the resources and the time to succeed or if every new initiative is rejected.

As a leader, you establish the environment in which your people think and work. The companies that surprise the market and their competitors are those that have a culture of risk and experimentation—and that culture is up to you.

11. The Principle of Economy

This principle refers to the importance of not expending any more men and matériel to achieve a military objective than it is worth or is necessary.

In business, the principle of economy means that you do everything at the lowest cost possible. You conduct a careful financial analysis before making any commitment. You conserve cash at all times. You continually look for ways to save money and reduce expenses.

Use your brainpower to replace financial power. Look for ways to accomplish your business goals in the most economic ways possible. There are two rules for financial success in business. Rule number one is, "Don't lose money!" Rule number two is, "Whenever you are tempted, refer back to rule number one."

Only spend money where it can have a direct influence on increasing sales or revenues. Don't spend money on non-revenue–generating expenses or activities until you have excessive cash reserves in the bank.

Treat your company like a turn-around at all times. Pretend that your company was on the verge of bankruptcy. What expenses would you curtail or discontinue? What steps would you take to ensure the survival of your business?

The key to success in business is to practice frugality at all times. Be careful with your money. Conserve it. Hoard it. Build up reserves. Always look for cheaper ways to accomplish the same task.

12. The Principle of Exploitation

This principle refers to the importance of the winning army taking full advantage of a victory.

Military commanders use the principle of exploitation when they achieve a breakthrough or a military advantage. They pour their entire army into the breakthrough or opportunity to gain as much ground as they possibly can.

In business, this means that you follow up and follow through when you achieve a market success or get a new customer.

As a business leader, encourage your people to never be satisfied with an initial victory or breakthrough. If a new product is successful, your product development and marketing teams should be rightly applauded and rewarded for their success. But they should also immediately begin to look for the next great product. One way to mandate this attitude as a leader is to require that the majority of your company's sales come from products introduced within the last five years.

If a customer is acquired, you should likewise encourage your sales people to sell all they can to that new customer or market. They should look for ways to up-sell and cross-sell more of your products and services by making the customer happy with his initial purchase decision. Once again, as a leader, you can either encourage or sabotage this behavior. Some leaders focus more on new customer numbers and less on customer retention rates, although it is far more expensive to acquire a new customer than to retain an existing one. As a result, their salespeople spend more time acquiring new customers and less time trying to keep the customers they have.

There are only three ways that your company can increase sales and revenues:

1. Sell to more *customers*. You accomplish this with better marketing, greater speed, more sales activity, and better sales training;

2. You can sell *more* to each customer. You accomplish this by up-selling the customer, or giving discounts on additional purchases, or

recommending add-ons to what you've already sold. Once you have a customer, as Shakespeare said, "Bind them to you with hoops of steel."

3. You can achieve *more frequent purchases* by each customer with special offers, well-targeted advertising, and special promotions.

The most cost-efficient ways to increase sales and revenues are numbers 2 and 3: exploit the customers you already have.

The Quality Service Strategy

The real key to the maximum exploitation and development of a customer, to getting the customer to buy more from you, is outstanding customer service.

The most important question in sales and customer service is, "Based on your experience with us, would you recommend us to others?"

It is 10 times easier to get a resale from a satisfied customer than to go out into the marketplace and get a brand new customer. It is 15 times easier to get a sale as the result of a referral than as the result of cold calling. Everything that your company can do to build customer loyalty increases your sales, resales, and referral business.

The most profitable companies have the highest levels of repeat sales and customer loyalty. What could you do, starting today, to achieve a strategy of preeminence where your customer sees you as the only supplier of what you sell?

The Great Law

The great law of the universe is the law of cause and effect. This law says that for every effect, there is a cause, or causes. Everything happens for a reason. Success is not an accident. Failure is not an accident.

The law of cause and effect says that if you do what other successful businesses do, you will eventually achieve the same results that other successful businesses do. But if you do not do what other successful businesses do, you will experience failure, frustration, and defeat in the marketplace.

The 12 principles covered in this chapter are seldom taught in business schools, only in military academies like West Point, Annapolis, Sandhurst, and L'Ecole Speciale Militaire de Saint-Cyr in France. It is interesting to note the large number of military officers from World War II who went on to head up major corporations, with great success, in later years. They found that the military principles of successful strategy were equally as applicable in corporate competition.

Thinking is the most important work you do as a leader. The better you think, the better decisions you will make. The better decisions you make, the better actions you will take. The better actions you take, the better results you will get. It all depends upon the quality of your thinking.

When you apply these military principles of strategy to your business, they will provide you with a series of thinking tools that you can use to achieve victory in your marketplace against determined competitors.

CHAPTER FOUR

Masterful Management!

"We're Overled and Undermanaged."

—HENRY MINTZBERG

Henry Mintzberg wrote in *Business Week* that too many leaders don't see themselves as managers. They believe that their job is "to do the right things," while others are responsible for "doing things right." That may look good in a consultant PowerPoint presentation or academic white paper, but the fact is that the best leaders are, first and foremost, managers. They make things happen. They get results. They organize people, allocate resources, implement strategies—whatever it takes to get things done. In *Execution*, Larry Bossidy writes, "Only the leader can make execution happen, through his or her deep personal involvement in the substance and even the details of execution."

The Seven Roles of the Manager

In any enterprise there are seven key roles of the manager. Each of them is only learned through trial and error and continuous practice. But they are all *learnable*, and they must be learned for you to realize your full potential as a leader.

One of the most important management qualities is *flexibility*. The more different mental tools and skills you have to get the most and the best out of your people, the more flexible and, therefore, the more effective you can be as a manager.

Each role is as important as any of the others. Norman Augustine, president of Martin Marietta, wrote, "The weakest important skill sets the height at which an executive can use all his other skills." Over the years, I have found that a person's weakest key skill determines the height of their income and the level of their success. An executive can be excellent in many areas, but the areas where he is weak will hold him back from achieving everything that is possible for him.

Give yourself a grade from 1 to 10 on each of these key roles. Be honest with yourself. And remember, they are all learnable with practice.

1. Planning

Planning is the process of determining exactly what is to be done.

Action without planning is the cause of every failure. Action preceded by thorough planning is usually the reason for every success.

Think on paper. Write down every detail of the goal or objective and every step you will have to take to achieve it.

Get the facts, especially the financial facts. Refuse to rely on guesswork or the hope that everything will turn out all right. Be mentally prepared to abandon the plan and try something else if you learn that it can't be done using the method you started with.

Just as there is an 80/20 rule, there is also a 10/90 rule that says, "The first 10 percent of the time you spend in planning often accounts for 90 percent of your success when you put your plan into action."

In business strategy, the purpose is to increase return on equity, or ROE. The goal of the company is to earn the very most possible on the amount of money invested in the business. In setting personal strategy, your goal is to increase "return on energy," the amount of mental, emotional, and physical energy that you invest to get results.

Because you save 10 minutes in execution for every minute you invest in planning, you achieve an ROE of 1000 percent by thinking through every critical detail before you begin.

The true measure of your planning ability is simple: Your plan works. As the result of your plan, you get the results you projected. If your plan doesn't work, you must change the plan until it does. One of the major reasons for failure as a leader is the inability or refusal to change plans from one that is failing to one that succeeds.

Remember the Six P Formula: *Proper Prior Planning Prevents Poor Performance.*

2. Organizing

Organizing is the process of assembling the people and resources you will need to fulfill the plan and achieve your goals.

This is a key skill of leadership. People with good organizational skills are invaluable to any organization. Nothing is possible without them.

In its simplest form, organization requires that you make a list of everything you will need to carry out the plan on schedule and on budget. These ingredients include money, people, offices, equipment, and technology. To ensure that you do not forget something essential, your list should be complete before you take action.

"For want of a nail, a horse was lost. For want of a horse, a rider was lost. For want of a rider, the battle was lost. From the loss of the battle, an empire was lost. Oh what a loss for one small nail!"

English proverb

Organize your list of requirements by sequence—what you need to do before you do something else, and by priority—what is more important and what is less important. Start on the most vital elements of your plan first.

Accept or assign clear responsibility for each task or activity. Practice the 20/80 rule of organization. This rule says that the first 20 percent of the time that you spend planning and organizing is as valuable, or more valuable, than the remaining 80 percent of tasks.

3. Staffing

You must attract and keep the people you need to carry out the plan and achieve the desired results.

Your ability to hire and keep the right people will account for as much as 95 percent of your ultimate success. Most of your frustrations and failures will be the result of having the wrong person in a key position.

Because this subject is so critical to your becoming an excellent leader, we will discuss it at length in chapter five.

4. Delegation

Delegation is the skill of assigning the right job to the right person in the right way.

You always have two choices: You can either do the job yourself, or you can get someone else to do it. Proper delegation is how you make sure that someone else does the job to an acceptable level of quality.

Your ability to delegate effectively is the key to leveraging yourself and multiplying your value to your company. Delegation allows you to move from what you can do personally to what you can manage.

Delegation is one of the most important management skills. Without the ability to delegate effectively and well, it is impossible for you to advance in management to higher positions of responsibility.

Delegation is not only about maximizing your own productivity and value; it is also about maximizing the productivity of your staff. Your job as a manager is to get the highest return on the company's investment in people. The average person today is working at 50 percent of capacity. With effective delegation, you can tap into that unused 50-percent potential to increase your staff's productivity.

Your job as a manager is to develop people. Delegation is the means that you use to bring out the very best in the people that you have.

The first step in delegation is to think through the job. Decide exactly what is to be done. What result do you want?

The second step in delegation is to set performance standards. How will you measure to determine whether the job has been done properly or not?

The third step is to determine a schedule and a deadline for getting the job done.

Task-Relevant Maturity

The task-relevant maturity of your staff—how long they have been on the job and how competent they are—determines your method of delegation.

Low task-relevant maturity means they are new and inexperienced in the job. In this case, use a directive delegation style. Tell people exactly what you want them to do.

Medium task-relevant maturity means staff have experience in the job; they know what they are doing. In this case, use the management by objectives delegation method. Tell people the end result that you want and then get out of their way and let them do it.

High task-relevant maturity is when the staff person is completely experienced and competent. Your method of delegation in this case is simply easy interaction.

The Art of Delegation

There are seven essentials for effective delegation:

1. Pick the right person. Picking the wrong person for a key task is a major reason for failure.

2. Match the requirements of the job to the abilities of the person. Be sure that the delegatee is capable of doing the job.

3. Delegate effectively to the right person. This frees you to do more things of higher value. The more of your essential tasks that you can teach and delegate to others, the greater the time you will have to do the things that only you can do.

4. Delegate smaller tasks to newer staff to build their confidence and competence.

5. Delegate the entire job. One hundred percent responsibility for a task is a major performance motivator. The more often you assign

responsibilities to the right people, the more competent they become.

6. Delegate clear outcomes. Make them measurable. If you can't measure it, you can't manage it. Explain what is to be done, how you think it should be done, and the reasons for doing this job in the first place.

7. Delegate with participation and discussion. Invite questions and be open to suggestions. There is a direct relationship between how much people are invited to talk about the job and how much they understand it, accept it, and become committed to it. You need to delegate in such a way that people walk away feeling, "This is my job; I own it."

Delegate authority over the resources staff will need to fulfill the responsibility. Be clear about the time they have, the money they can spend, and the people they can call on to help them to do the job.

Practice *management by exception* when you delegate. Set clear goals, standards, and deadlines for the delegated task. A job without a deadline is merely a discussion. Then tell people to come back to you only if they have a problem. If they are on schedule and on budget, they do not need to report. You can assume that they have the job under control.

Delegation is the key skill to growing your people. When you become effective at delegating with a few staff members, you will soon be given more people to delegate to, plus greater responsibilities, as a result of your delegation skills.

All excellent managers are excellent delegators. In old-school thinking, people used to say that, "If you want the job done right, you have to do it yourself."

In new-school thinking, however, the correct statement is, "If you want the job done right, you have to delegate it properly to others so that they can do it to the proper standard."

5. Supervising

Supervising is the process of making sure the job is done on time and on budget. Delegation is not abdication; you are still accountable for results. The more important the job is, the more important it is that you keep on top of it.

The job of the manager is to get things done through *others.* Your ability to organize the work and to supervise your staff effectively to get the job done on schedule and on budget is the key to getting the results for which you are responsible.

Your ability to supervise others can be greatly improved by learning what other excellent managers have discovered over the years and by applying these principles and ideas to your interactions with your subordinates.

The Factory Model

The application of the factory model of productivity to people, departments, and companies is a useful management tool.

Inputs go into the factory—time, money, supplies, equipment, supervision, and training. In the factory, production activities are performed. The results of the process come out of the factory.

Average people tend to focus on their job's activities. Leaders focus instead on the outputs and results expected of the process.

In operating your "factory," your job is to increase the quality and quantity of output relative to input. Plan the work in advance to ensure maximum use of human resources, your most costly input. Make sure that each person is working on the most valuable use of their time most of the time.

To supervise well, you must be clear about the key result areas for a job, which are always objective, measurable, and time-bounded. What specific results do you want him or her to achieve at each stage of the work?

What are the tasks that he must do well to be successful in his job? Why is he on the payroll? What can only he do that, done well, will make a real contribution to your business? Excellent executives always focus on the strengths and the best talents and abilities of each person.

Once you have defined a key result area, you have to set standards of performance for that part of the job. Every person has to know exactly what you expect to be done, when it should be done, and to what standard. Knowing what is expected is a major performance motivator.

One of your responsibilities with your staff is to define performance so that they can recognize it and work toward it. Only excellent performance motivates people and releases their potential. What gets measured gets done! If you can't measure it, you can't do it effectively.

Check on the Job

It's not enough to set standards and then walk away. As supervisor, you must make sure that the work is being done correctly. One of the best supervision techniques is management-by-wandering-around, when the manager is out and among the staff on a regular basis, keeping his fingers on the pulse of the business. By wandering around, you get immediate and timely feedback about the work and can act quickly to solve problems or make changes.

The Best Managers

According to numerous surveys of employees in the work world, the best bosses and supervisors possess three qualities:

1. **Structure.** Everyone knows exactly what needs to be done, why it is to be done, and to what standard.

2. **Consideration.** The boss makes employees feel that he or she really cares about them.

3. **Freedom.** Good bosses give their people freedom to perform. Once they have assigned a task, they try to stay out of the way, except to comment and to help when needed.

Back to School

One of your jobs as the leader is to be a teacher. The reason you are in charge is because of your superior level of knowledge and skill. One of the most helpful things you do is to pass on your knowledge and skill to those who report to you.

Teach other people how to do the job that you have already mastered. You multiply your output by teaching someone else how to do something that only you can do. And you increase their value to the business.

Five Keys to Excellent Supervision

There are five keys to excellent supervision.

1. Accept complete responsibility for your staff. You choose them, you assign them, and you manage them.

2. Look upon your staff with the same patience and understanding as you would look upon younger members of your family.

3. Practice the Friendship Factor with them, which is composed of three components: time, caring, and respect. Give staff time when they want to talk. Express caring and concern for them and their problems. Treat them with respect, the same way you would treat a customer or friend.

4. Practice Servant Leadership, by seeing your job as a position of trust with your subordinates. Just as they are there to serve you and the company, you are there to serve them, as well.

5. Practice Golden Rule Management. Treat each person the way you would like to be treated if the situation were reversed. When you practice Golden Rule Management—you manage other people the way you would like to be managed—you will elicit better performance from your people than in any other way.

6. Measuring

Measuring requires setting metrics—measures and numbers—for each part of the work, including setting standards of performance for each job.

Every business activity can be expressed and defined in numbers of some kind, typically financial numbers.

In Jim Collins's book *Good to Great*, he emphasizes the importance of the economic denominator in any business. This is sometimes referred to as a Critical Success Factor (CSF), the measure of which is the best indicator of the health of the business, or of some part of the business.

With each job, or part of a job, some kind of measure can be attached to it. In sales, the measure can be the number of calls, or the number of face-to-face appointments. If it is the leadership of the company, the critical measure can be quarterly sales, profitability, or the share price. In business, the ultimate number is usually *net cash flow*, the actual amount of free cash that is available—after all charges—to pay out as profits and dividends.

You must establish numbers for yourself in each key area. These become your targets, and measures of how well you are doing. Above all, you must select one number that is more indicative of your success than any other, and focus on that number every day.

In the same way, every person who works for you must have a number, or numbers, to focus on in their work. Each day, manage by checking to see how closely the person is coming to hitting those numbers.

The Hawthorne principle says that whenever people are clear about a particular number and focus on it, their performance in the area measured by that number improves.

All rewards, recognition, promotion, and bonuses in your company should be tied to performance, to achieving the numbers and measures you have set.

7. Reporting

You must keep the key people inside and outside of your business informed at all times.

This is one of the most important responsibilities of leadership—and of people at every level of the organization. Fully 95 percent of problems in a company can be traced back to poor or nonexistent communications. People were not informed of events or given information that was essential to their ability to do their jobs correctly.

Do you know who needs to know your results? Who needs to know what you are doing so that they can do their jobs properly? Who is going to be unhappy if you do or fail to do something and they don't know about it? When in doubt, more information is better than less information.

Make a list of everyone who needs to know what you are doing and how well you are doing it. Start with your boss. What information does your boss need from you on a regular basis? Go and ask. Write it down. Report back regularly.

Especially if there is bad news, be sure that you tell it first. If someone else conveys the negative information, it can easily get distorted and reflect badly on you before you even get a chance to comment. Practice a "no surprises" strategy. As we used to say as kids, "Beat the news home!"

Knowing how to report to your boss is a key skill of managing up. Leadership is not just about managing down—managing your employees and subordinates—it is also about managing your boss. The same basic rules of communication and reporting apply. Give those you report to honest and complete information and speak with candor. Don't be afraid to suggest initiatives and to campaign hard for what you believe. To get things done, you not only need your employees to buy in to your goals, you need your boss to buy in as well.

Don't Forget the Staff

Your boss is not the only person you need to inform. Identify the other people in and outside your business who need information from you to do their jobs properly or to make good decisions. Ask them what information they need, how often, and in what form.

Make sure that your staff and subordinates are kept fully informed about everything that affects their jobs. Hold regular meetings, preferably every week, to review progress and keep them up to date.

In times of crisis, you need to meet more often, sometimes every day, to keep people informed and stop them from wondering or worrying.

Choose How to Communicate

A key element of reporting effectively involves the medium that you use. People are either visual (70 percent) or auditory (30 percent). Visual people need to see the information written down. If they don't see it, they don't remember it or they remember it incorrectly. If you tell something to a visual person, he will ask, "Do you have that in writing?"

Auditory people like to talk and to hear the information. They are not as interested in reading it. If you present a written report to an auditory person, he will glance at it and ask you, "What does it say?"

Start by determining if your boss is visual or auditory. Ask her how she likes to receive information and then report accordingly. Ask your colleagues and staff members how they like to receive information, and be sure that you present your reports in a form that they can understand.

Finally, set up a regular schedule for reporting, especially on important activities. Prepare an agenda for each meeting. Invite questions, and be sure that everyone understands what is going on. This approach can save you a fortune in lost time and unnecessary expense.

Communication is one of the key responsibilities of leaders and managers. We'll learn more about communication in chapter eight.

The Seven Determinants of Business Success

There are seven key factors that are relevant to every business and organization. A failure or a shortcoming in any one of these areas can lead to the collapse of the enterprise. Your job as a leader and a manager is to ensure that your company succeeds in each of these areas. The roles and skills described above will help you achieve the results described below.

1. Productivity

Every business is subject to the laws of economics. The ultimate goal of business activity is profits, an excess of income over costs. In tough markets, the low cost leader has a distinct advantage over its competitors. Look at WalMart.

In the simplest terms, the key to higher levels of productivity from invested assets is to do more with less, to continually find ways to deliver the same quality and quantity of goods and services at lower costs.

In tough times, with tight markets and aggressive competitors, your ability to cut costs can make the difference between success and failure. Here is the rule: Whatever cutbacks you would be willing to make if the survival of your business were at stake, make them immediately. Don't wait until the last minute. It might be too late.

Invite Ideas and Suggestions

Ask everyone in your business for ideas and suggestions to reduce expenses without compromising the quality of your product or service. Delay and defer all nonessential expenditures. Lease rather than buy; rent rather than lease; borrow rather than rent. Use your imagination and ingenuity to get more done at a lower cost.

Apply the zero-based thinking principle to every cost and activity. Ask, "If we were not spending this amount in this area or doing things this way already, would we start doing this again today, based on the current situation?"

View your business through the eyes of a turnaround specialist. If your business was on the brink of bankruptcy, what costs would you cut, and how fast?

2. Customer Satisfaction

Customer satisfaction is the key determinant of long-term business success.

The purpose of a business is to create and keep a customer. Profits are what you earn by creating and keeping customers in sufficient quantities and in a cost-effective way.

The primary focus of a successful business must be customer satisfaction. This is the only way to ensure that customers will return and keep buying your products and services. As a leader and manager, make sure everyone in the company is focused on this goal.

The key measure of customer satisfaction is repeat business. This means that customers are so happy with their experience with the product or service they purchased that they buy again and again. Repeat sales have the lowest cost and the highest profit margins of all.

The Ultimate Question

The most important measure of customer satisfaction, according to Fred Reichhold in his book *The Ultimate Question*, is the answer to the question, "Would you recommend us to others?"

The totality of the customer experience with your product, your people, and your services can be summed up in your customer's response to this question.

Ask your customers to rate your company on a scale of 1 to 10 on this question. According to Reichhold's research, those customers giving you a grade of 9 or 10 represent 85 percent of your repeat customers and referrals.

Achieving a high score on this question has become the number that many companies use to evaluate each person and function in the business. When companies concentrate on improving this score, their sales and profits begin to increase rapidly.

If you were to commission an independent company to survey customers and ask which companies in your industry give the best customer service, how do you think your company would rank? Whatever the answer, what actions could you take, starting today, to improve your ranking?

Everything you do to increase customer satisfaction builds customer loyalty and generates repeat business. In today's marketplace, this must be a central focus of business leadership.

3. Profitability

This is the true measure of leadership—the only way to evaluate the efficiency with which money and people are used in a business.

The law of concentration says, "Whatever you dwell upon, grows in your experience." Every person in your business should be focused on profitability, all the time.

Baron de Rothschild, in his *Maxims for Business Success*, said, "Always focus on net profits."

As it happens, because many companies aggregate the expenses of marketing, administration, accounting, and outside services into a lump figure, they do not know for sure how much actual profit they earn on each particular product. Every leader should know the true profitability of every product or service in his or her company. If you don't, conduct a profit analysis on your business. List each product or service you offer, and determine exactly how much net profit each of them earns per sale, and in total. Then apply the 80/20 rule, introduced in the previous chapter, to all products and services. What are the 20 percent of your products and services that generate 80 percent of your profits? If you were forced to cut back to your most profitable products, which ones would you hold onto the tightest?

Identify the 20 percent of your customers who purchase 80 percent of your products and services. Then determine the 20 percent of your customers who are the most profitable for you. Often, these customer groups are not the same.

Customer Acquisition Costs

Also apply the 80/20 rule to your sales and marketing activities. What are the 20 percent of marketing and sales methods that generate 80 percent of your sales and revenues?

Whatever your industry, you are in the business of "buying" customers. Every customer you buy has both a cost of acquisition and a cost of fulfillment. The cost of acquisition includes all of your marketing and sales costs. What is your cost of customer acquisition? How much do you pay, directly and indirectly, to get a new customer? How much does it cost to keep that customer? Most companies have no idea.

You succeed in business to the degree that your total costs of acquiring and satisfying a customer are lower than the amount you receive for what you sell. Based on this, what are your most profitable methods of customer acquisition?

Finally, what are your most profitable business activities? What are the things that your company does that yield the highest net profit, both in the short term and in the long term? What are the most profitable things that you do personally? What are the most profitable activities of your key people?

Whatever your answers to the above questions, a key responsibility of leadership is to focus and concentrate your limited resources on those areas and activities where the highest net profits are possible.

4. Quality

Achieving and maintaining high quality standards relative to your competitors is a key to business survival.

In any market, the company that has the highest quality rating is usually the most profitable. What is the rating of your company? If you were to be compared to each of your competitors, how would informed customers in your marketplace rank you? Who are you better than? Who is better than you? What can you do about it?

In the mind of the customer, quality is composed of two factors: the product or service itself and the way it is sold, delivered, and serviced.

The quality of a product or service is determined by how often and dependably that it does what you said it would do when you sold it.

The quality of your services is determined by how well (or poorly) your customers are treated personally by people in your company.

Because of the Hawthorne principle described earlier in this chapter, making quality improvement a major focus in your company triggers an unending stream of ideas to improve everything you do for and with your customers.

Sometimes one great idea for improving your customers' perception of the quality your company delivers can enable you to sell far more in a competitive market. One improvement in your product or service can give you a customer satisfaction edge. One improvement in the way you deal with your customers can get them coming back to you over and over again.

5. Innovation

Many management experts feel that innovation is the key to business success. They are probably right. With rapid increases in information, continuous breakthroughs in technology, and determined world-wide competition, your ability to innovate quickly is essential to your survival.

Create a culture of innovation in your company so that everyone continually strives to develop new and better products and services, as well as new and better ways to operate, market and sell, and improve customer service. Be open to new ideas and suggestions. Be open to trials and errors. Reward initiative.

Focus on the Customer

The focus on the customer is indispensable. Continually ask what the customer will want tomorrow. What are his needs, concerns, fears, frustrations?

The biggest danger of business success is that it leads to complacency. People become satisfied and reluctant to change, to rock the boat. This is especially dangerous if the leader is complacent. Are you self-satisfied and content? Do you believe that your organization will survive and thrive by continuing to do what it has been doing—that nothing needs to change? Are you afraid to take chances or to let your people take chances? If so, you are setting your company up for a downfall.

Sources of Innovation

The unexpected successes and the unexpected failures in your business are the major sources of innovation. A product can sell far more than you anticipated, or far less. In either case, this means that something is different in your market and in your customer's situation. What do you need to do to change your offerings or to expand and exploit a larger market?

Innovation is about the future. Fully 20 percent of your products and services will be obsolete within a couple of years, and maybe even faster. What are you going to replace them with? The opportunities of tomorrow will always be different from the markets of today.

In chapter seven, I will share some of the best techniques for creative thinking and problem solving ever discovered. These techniques will help you discover new opportunities for innovation in your company—opportunities you never knew existed.

6. Organizational Development

Continually seek ways to get better results by reorganizing people and resources, moving them to where they can produce better results for your business.

There are three *Rs* you can use regularly to ensure that your company is functioning at the highest levels of efficiency and effectiveness:

1. Restructuring. This is the process of moving people and resources to higher profit areas. Focus more of your best people and time on the 20 percent of activities that generate 80 percent of your sales and profits.

2. Reengineering. Stand back and look at your entire work process. How could you simplify the work so that you can produce your products and satisfy your customers faster?

Make a list of every job and function that is performed in the course of your business activities. Go over the list of steps and look for ways to reduce them. Perhaps you could consolidate several jobs held by different people and make one person responsible for that newly combined job.

Perhaps you could expand the definition of a job and have one person be responsible for all of it rather than dividing it up.

Identify the tasks you do internally that could be outsourced to a company that specializes in that area and could probably do it faster and cheaper. Especially, how can you convert fixed costs into variable costs and lower your monthly break-even point?

Finally, be prepared to completely eliminate certain tasks, activities, and even staff. Often there are things you are doing today that seemed like a good idea when you began them. Now, with the passing of time, you find that they are both expensive and unnecessary. It is time to cut them back, or eliminate them completely.

3. Reinventing. Imagine walking across the street and starting your business or career over again. What would you immediately start up again? What products or services would you immediately begin marketing and selling? What products and services would you no longer offer? Which business expenses or activities would you get into again, and which would you discontinue?

When you develop a "reinvention" way of looking at your world, you will see many opportunities to reorganize your life and improve your ways of doing business. You will find yourself doing more and more of those things that represent the highest levels of profitability, and letting the rest go.

7. People-Building

Almost all companies say, "Our people are our most important asset." But only a few companies treat their employees as if they really believe it. The spoken accolades of a leader ring false when his actions show that he doesn't respect or trust his people.

The fact is that most people in your company today are *knowledge* workers. They work with their minds. They can only be measured by the results they get at their jobs.

How people think and feel about their companies, their jobs, their managers, and their coworkers determine the quality and quantity of their work. These things cannot be left to chance.

Look for ways to increase loyalty and build both the competence and self-esteem of your staff and your key people.

Release Individual Potential

The average person works at 50 percent or less of his or her potential. This means that the greatest improvements in performance and results can come from unlocking and unleashing the latent potential in each person who reports to you.

However, all motivation is self-motivation. The manager cannot motivate anyone. What he can do is to create an environment where motivation happens naturally. This requires simultaneously putting all the known motivators in place while *removing* the demotivators that inhibit performance.

The best organizations in every industry are far more productive and profitable than average organizations in the same industry. They are characterized by high trust environments where people feel good about themselves and what they do. People are motivated when they feel terrific about themselves. The measure? When people say, "This is a great place to work!"

Building and maintaining a high trust environment is one of the most important things that you can possibly do as a leader, especially in times of uncertainty. Your job as an executive is to bring out the best in your people. People perform best when they feel safe, secure, and respected by you and the people around them, and when they feel appreciated, valued, and trusted.

Chapter five, hiring and keeping people, offers some specific ways to keep people motivated and performing.

Build Self-Esteem

The key to motivation, enthusiasm, and a positive self-image is the individual's level of self-esteem.

Self-esteem has best been defined as how much you like yourself. The more you like and respect yourself, the better you perform in every area. The more you like yourself, the more you like others and the better you get along with them.

The more you like yourself, the bigger the goals you set for yourself and the longer you persist in the pursuit of those goals. The more you like yourself, the higher the standards you set for yourself and the better the work you do. Self-esteem is the core emotion that companies must reinforce and encourage to create a great place to work.

The opposites of self-esteem are fear, insecurity, negativity, feelings of inferiority, and poor human relations. Fear and doubt have always been the greatest enemies of human happiness and performance.

Fear of any kind undermines, and even paralyzes, performance. Fear depresses your personality and undermines your effectiveness. Fear of failure is the greatest single obstacle to success in adult life. Fear of failure leads to self-doubt, and self-doubt causes people to hold back, to hesitate, to sell themselves short.

The second major cluster of fears revolves around the fear of rejection. This is the fear of disapproval, ridicule, embarrassment, and, especially, the fear of criticism.

These fears lie just below the surface of the personality of the average person, just waiting to be triggered by something that someone, especially the boss, says or implies. These fears are easily triggered by a look, a glance, or a negative response to a situation at work.

Drive out Fear

What is the key to creating a high trust environment? Drive out fear!

Resolve to eliminate criticism of all kinds from your vocabulary. Assume the best of intentions on the part of others. Allow honest mistakes. Don't react or overreact when things do not go as you expected.

Build and reinforce self-esteem on every occasion. Tell people how good they are. Build positive self-images with regular recognition, rewards, and approval. Take time to express compassion, concern, and caring for each person.

Apologize early and often. If you say or do something that triggers the fears of failure or rejection in another person, go and say, "I'm sorry, I shouldn't have said that." Take back the destructive criticism.

Dedicate yourself to creating an environment where people feel terrific about themselves. Drive out fear. Create a high trust environment, so that everybody who works with you says, "This is a great place to work!"

In the next chapter on hiring and keeping the best people, we'll learn more about the secrets of building a high trust work environment and keeping people motivated and engaged.

Competence Is at the Heart of Success

Competence is at the heart of every successful manager or leader. Without competence, you can neither lead nor manage. You can't manage because you don't have the skills to do what has to be done. And you can't lead because you haven't earned the respect of those around you.

You don't have to be the smartest person in the room. In fact, the best leaders are those who have the confidence to surround themselves with the best people in the business. It's the insecure leader who hires people who will just smile and nod at everything the leader says.

But there is a difference between being the smartest person in the company and being incompetent. If you can't make decisions or you make the wrong decisions continuously, you will lose the confidence of those around you and fail as a leader. Leadership expert Michael Useem tells the true story of a firefighting crew chief leading a group of men battling a huge forest fire in the mountains. Because of several problematic decisions made earlier, many of the men started to doubt the competence of their chief. When the fire suddenly shifted toward the firefighters, the crew chief found a way to save the men from death. But the men no longer trusted the chief; as a result, the chief survived, but most of his men died.

To fulfill your potential, you must become excellent at what you do.

Resolve to be the best, to join the top 10 percent in your field. Set your standards high. Look around you at the best people in your business; think about how you could be as good as or better at your job than they are.

The good news is that all business skills are learnable through practice and repetition. The top people in every field got there by continually working on themselves, often for many years, before they finally broke from the pack and moved ahead. And what others have learned and done, you can, within reason, do as well.

Choose your personal area of excellence, your unique selling proposition, the factor or factors that make you special. Just as a company and product must be excellent and special in some way to stand out in a competitive market, so must you. Your decision to excel in a particular area moves you into the top 10 percent in your field, because most people never make that decision in their entire careers.

The key to moving from good to great in your field is to ask yourself the brutal question: "Why aren't I already the best at what I do?" The answer is always the same. The reason you are not at the top of your field is because you have not yet decided to be there, or you have not backed that decision up with the hard, hard work on yourself that is necessary.

Hire and Keep the Best People

"Formal education will make you a living; self education will make you a fortune."

—JIM ROHN

Your skill in hiring and keeping the best people will determine your success as a leader more than any other single factor.

The ability to attract and motivate excellent people who can help you build your business is a critical constraint on the growth and success of your business, or any business. Everything else can be acquired somewhere. You can get all the capital, real estate, furniture, fixtures, manufacturing and distribution equipment, packaging, and marketing materials you need. But what makes everything work is the people behind them—and there has never been such an extreme shortage of quality people as we are experiencing today.

In Jim Collins's bestselling book *Good to Great,* he writes that the key to building a great company is to "Get the right people on the bus, get the wrong people off the bus, and then get the right people in the right seats on the bus."

In Larry Bossidy's bestselling book *Execution,* he writes that the key to business success is to find people who can execute and who can get the job done quickly and well.

The skill of hiring and keeping good people is not genetic. No one is born with it. It is a skill that, like any other business skill, can be learned with practice. By practicing the ideas in this chapter, you can dramatically increase your effectiveness at finding and keeping the best people for your business.

Employers today have to make a major mental paradigm shift. We have to direct our attention to hiring and keeping good people and focus on that as a major responsibility of management. It may be the most important thing we learn to do.

Select the Right People

The selection process is the key to your success and to the success of your company. Nothing is more important to your future than your ability to select the right people to work with you to make that future a reality.

Unfortunately, very few managers have been thoroughly trained in the process of personnel selection. As a result, much of selection is done on the basis of intuition, gut feelings, and seat-of-the-pants reasoning. But this approach is not for you.

The rule is that if you select in haste, you will repent at leisure. Many of the worst problems in business result from having hired a person too quickly and then having to wrestle with the decision and deal with all the problems that came along with it.

As a manager, you are responsible for spending the time and the effort required to make a good hire. As a leader, you have two responsibilities. One is to enable your managers to make the best decisions. Don't set deadlines for new hires unless you absolutely have to. As we'll see below, taking your time is one of the keys to successful recruitment.

Your second responsibility is to be involved in the hiring of employees at all levels in your organization. You may not do initial interviews for some employees, but no employees should be hired before you have seen and talked to them.

Hire Slowly and Fire Fast

One of the rules for good hiring is this: Hire slowly and fire fast. The very best time to fire a person is the first time it crosses your mind. If you have made a poor selection decision, don't compound the decision by keeping the wrong person in place. Have the courage and common sense to admit that you have made a mistake; then correct the mistake and get on with business.

In management, your natural tendency is to hire a person as a solution to a problem, to fill a hole in the lineup, or to do a job that suddenly needs to be done. This is like grabbing a bucket of water and throwing it on a fire. Sometimes, if you are not careful, the bucket turns out to be full of gasoline, and the situation you created can be worse than the situation you are trying to correct.

Ask yourself honestly: Have I ever hired a person quickly, with little forethought? How often have you had problems as a result? There is nothing wrong with making a mistake, as long as you learn from the mistake and do not repeat it.

Hiring is an art. It cannot be rushed. All people decisions require a good deal of thought and reflection before you make them. Fast hiring decisions usually turn out to be wrong hiring decisions.

A manager told me once that he had a simple rule for hiring anyone. Once he had decided upon the candidate, he waited for 30 days before he made the final offer. He found that the very act of delaying a hiring decision made it a vastly better decision when he finally came around to it.

The Cost of Haste

Poor personnel selection is very expensive. First is your lost time: the time that you spent interviewing, hiring, and training people to get them up to speed.

Then there is your lost money: the salary and training expenses for the person who eventually doesn't work out.

Finally, there is lost productivity while you are busy finding a replacement for the person you shouldn't have hired in the first place.

The rule is that it costs about three times a person's annual salary to hire the wrong person and to replace them. If you hire a person for $50,000 a year who does not work out, the overall cost to you and the company will be about $150,000. It therefore behooves you to think carefully before you bring a new person on board. Sometimes the best hiring decision you ever make is the one you decide not to make in the first place.

Think the Job Through

Before you begin your search for new employees, take time to think the job through carefully, or make sure that the managers who will be hiring staff have themselves carefully thought through the job. The advice below should be followed closely by anyone involved in hiring employees for your company, whether it's the CEO looking for a VP of finance or the facilities manager hiring a new maintenance person.

First, remember the 10/90 rule I mentioned earlier. This rule says that the initial 10 percent of time that you spend thinking and planning will save you 90 percent of the time and effort required to make the right decision and get the long-term right result.

Think through the exact output responsibilities of the job.

Imagine that the job is a pipeline. What exactly comes out of the other end of the pipeline in terms of the results that the person is expected to accomplish? Think in terms of results rather than activities. Think in terms of outputs rather than inputs.

Imagine that you are going to buy a specific quality and quantity of results in the marketplace. You are receiving these results in exchange for the money that you are willing, in the form of salary, to pay. Exactly what will these results look like?

Think on Paper

Think through what the person is expected to accomplish, day in and day out. Describe a typical workday and work week, from morning to night. The clearer you are about the job that is to be done, the easier it will be for you to find the best candidate for the job.

Once you have determined the required results, identify the exact skills that the ideal candidate will require in order to achieve those results. Many companies believe in hiring for personality and attitude and then teaching the specific skills. But you should demand a certain demonstrated skill level from the very beginning, if you want to hire the best people.

Identify the ideal personal attributes or qualities that the candidate will have. You will especially want someone who is honest, positive, hard-working, energetic, focused, and open-minded. Write these qualities down and organize them in terms of their importance to you and to the job.

Now try to think of anything else that the perfect person for the job would bring. It could be as complex as a certain experience (for example, extensive international travel) or as mundane as his or her address (you prefer people who live close to the workplace). Think about the people with whom the person will be working. Everyone has to fit into a team. It's absolutely essential that whomever you hire will get along with, and be accepted by, the other staff.

Finally, be sure that a single person can do the job you are hiring for. Sometimes, with rapid change, the job may have grown so complex that you need two different people with two different sets of skills and attributes to do it properly.

Once you have listed everything you can think of to describe the ideal candidate, circulate this list to other people who will be working with the candidate. Finalize the list together, then prioritize the items on the list. In the end, you will have a terrific description of the ideal person.

You can now write a description of the job.

Write Out the Job Description

Start the job description by standing back and thinking about what the individual will be doing from the time he or she starts in the morning until the time he or she finishes in the evening. Think of the job as a production process, and identify each step in the production process as a task that must be completed to a minimum standard of performance. Write it down.

List every job function and responsibility that the individual will have, from arriving in the morning to checking messages and responding to telephone calls and e-mail all the way through to measuring and reporting on progress to his or her superior. Don't leave anything out.

Once you have a description of the ideal candidate and a clear description of everything that the candidate will be expected to do, set priorities on both lists. Divide the lists into *Musts* and *Wants*. Some qualities and output responsibilities will be absolutely essential to the successful completion of the job. Some are quite desirable but not absolutely essential.

With the ideal candidate description and clear job description in hand, you are now ready to cast your net and begin finding the right person for the job.

Find Suitable Candidates

It used to be that we would start looking for a person when we had an opening or a need for that person. Today, however, you must be in a permanent hiring mode. You must scan your world like radar scans the horizon, continually looking for more and better people to work for you. It is a never-ending job, the success of which will largely determine your success as an executive.

An important part of the selection process is generating a sufficient pool of suitable candidates from which to choose. There are several places for you to find people.

The first place is from within your own staff and personnel department. Conduct an internal search for the kind of person you are looking for. Offer the job to existing staff first if you possibly can.

Many companies today offer hiring bonuses to their staff who find a person who matches a particular description. The average person knows about 300 other people by their first names. When everyone on your staff knows that you are looking for a particular type of person, they will all become alert to locating that kind of person in the course of their activities.

Another great source is your personal contacts. Fully 85 percent of new people come through references and referrals from others. Once you have a written job description, get in touch with everyone you know who might run across the kind of person you are seeking.

Tell your customers, your bankers, your suppliers, your friends, your contacts, your acquaintances, and even people with whom you deal on an occasional basis, such as your lawyers, accountants, business associates, and so on. Cast your net as widely as possible.

Other excellent sources of high quality candidates are executive recruiters and placement agencies. Depending on the size of your business, executive recruiters and placement agencies can save you an enormous amount of time, money, and effort sorting through and finding the kind of people you need to help you grow your business.

Newspaper ads are another source of candidates but usually the least effective source. The Sunday job section is best. The key is a specific job description in the ad and then pre-screening people who phone based on the requirements that you have published. Fully 85 percent of people who respond to newspaper ads are not suitable, and they can be sorted out on the telephone during the initial contact.

Perhaps the most important and fastest growing source of job candidates is the Internet. One-eighth of new jobs today are already being filled from Internet advertising, up from zero just a few years ago. The Internet sites devoted to helping companies find good people, such as Craigslist, Monster.com, and Career Track, are fast, efficient, and inexpensive, and they reach all over the country.

Interview Effectively

Most executives have never been taught how to properly interview people for a position. Fortunately, the process is quite simple, as long as you can discipline yourself to learn it and then follow it each time.

Start by putting the candidate at ease and helping him or her to relax. Tell him or her that this is just an exploratory interview and that your mutual goal is to see if what you are offering and what the candidate is looking for is the same thing.

Don't start selling until you have decided to buy. In other words, resist the temptation to convince the candidate that this is a great job, and a great company, before you have concluded that this is the kind of person that you want in the first place.

What to Look For

Here are some things to look for. First of all, look for achievement or result orientation. When you ask questions and listen to the answers, look for examples in the person's background where he or she really enjoyed succeeding and getting results at a job.

Past performance in the workplace is the very best indicator of what the candidate is likely to do in the job that you are offering. Ask questions about his or her previous successes. Especially, ask about his or her greatest achievement in the world of work. Probe this answer, and ask why he or she feels so good about that accomplishment.

Another thing to watch for is intelligent questions. One of the hallmarks of intelligence is curiosity. A good candidate demonstrates curiosity with a series of questions, usually written out, that he or she will want to ask about you, the company, the job, the opportunities for the future, and so on.

Especially, look for a sense of urgency. A good question you can ask is, "If we were to offer you this job, how soon would you be ready to start?" The right candidate will want to start as soon as possible. The wrong candidate will have all kinds of reasons for procrastinating or delaying leaving his or her current employer.

When you read the candidate's resume, look for simplicity, honesty, and a focus on accomplishments and achievements rather than a description of activities and length of time in the job. What you are looking for is *transferability of results*.

Be careful about reference letters. They are often useless or

HOW THE BEST LEADERS LEAD

deceptive. Phone the writers of reference letters personally. Many companies today will not tell you anything about a previous employee for fear of being sued. In this case, you can always ask this question, "Would you hire this person back again today if he applied to you for a job?" All this requires is a simple "Yes" or "No" and is not an actionable response. If he would not hire the person back, that's a red flag on the candidate.

There is a simple formula you can use in an interview to know if the right person is in front of you. It is called the Swan Formula and is based on the letters that stand for the four things you are looking for: Smart, Works Hard, Ambitious, and Nice.

Remember, quick personnel decisions are almost invariably wrong personnel decisions. Go slowly. Be patient. Ask good questions and listen carefully to the answers. Take notes when the person talks. Ask questions that revolve around the highest priority items on your job description. Ask the candidate questions about how he or she feels that he or she would perform in those areas.

Only when you have reached the conclusion that this is the kind of person that you would like should you tell him or her more details about the company and the job. Only start selling when you have decided to buy.

Practice the Law of Three

This powerful technique can dramatically improve your ability to select the right people for the long term. Follow the law of three. Interview at least three candidates for any position. Interview the candidate that you like the most at least three times. Interview the candidate that you like the most in at least three different locations.

Hiring decisions that you make by intuition can often turn out to be unsuccessful. But when you interview three different candidates for the job, you get a better feeling for which of the candidates would be best. You get a better sense of what is available and exactly what it is you want. If you only speak to one person, your range of possibilities is too limited.

Never offer the person the job at the first interview. If you like him or her, invite him or her back for a second and third interview. Remember, the best the candidate will ever appear will be at the first interview. At the second interview, you will see and experience a different person. At the third interview, the person may be so completely different that you will wonder what you were thinking when you interviewed him or her the first time.

Finally, interview the person in at least three different locations. Interview him once in your office, once down the hall or in a separate room, and perhaps once across the street at a coffee shop. A person who looks good in your office may look average down the hall and completely mediocre when taken out for coffee or lunch. Remember, the slower you go, the better decisions you will make.

The final application of the law of three is to have the candidate interviewed by at least three other potential coworkers. Don't rely exclusively on your own judgment in hiring someone. A person that you may like initially may turn out to be completely unacceptable when other people have a chance to express their opinions.

In my company, everyone gets a chance to interview a new candidate, and then everyone votes on that candidate before he or she receives a job offer. It is absolutely amazing what the candidate will reveal when he speaks to a potential coworker as opposed to a potential boss.

Select Properly

Before you make the final hiring decision, there are some key things that you can do. First of all, consider the corporate climate and the people mix in your company. This plays a vital part in the new employee's future performance. Will he or she fit in to your corporate culture and climate? Will he or she be happy in your business? This is very important.

Use the "family member" method of selection. Ask yourself, "Would I feel comfortable inviting this person to my home to have dinner with my family on Sunday night?" This great question gives you a very reliable inner sense of whether or not this person will fit in with you and others.

Would you put your son or daughter to work with or under this person? If not, why not? When you imagine assigning one of your children to work under this person, you get a much clearer picture of whether or not this person is appropriate for your business for the long term.

Finally, do you genuinely like this person? You should only hire people who you like and enjoy. Would you be comfortable working with this person for the next 20 years? Remember, long-term vision dramatically improves short-term decision making.

Now review your feelings with other people who will be working with this person. Listen to them carefully, and then take some time by yourself to decide whether or not this is the right person for you.

A friend of mine went through an exhaustive hiring process; he interviewed 35 candidates, many of them several times. At the end of the process, he decided not to hire any of them. After years of experience, he has learned that a bad hiring decision is worse than no hiring decision at all.

Negotiate the Right Salary

With regard to salary, bonuses, and other forms of compensation, remember this key rule: "Good people are free."

Good people are *free* in that they contribute more in dollar value than you pay them in salary and bonuses. Every good person that you add to your payroll increases your bottom line. The profitability of your company is largely determined by your ability to attract and keep good people who contribute far more than they take out. For this reason, the amount you pay should largely be determined by the potential contribution of the other person, not some arbitrary rules in the marketplace or in your industry.

The rule today is that you have to pay talented people whatever it takes to get them, based on what they could get working for someone else in another company. However, the better prepared you are for a salary negotiation, the better the deal you will make. Know what the job is worth in the current market, know what you can afford to pay, and get an idea of what the candidate will accept (for example, ask, "How much money do you have to make to feel comfortable at this job?").

If you are hiring someone away from another company, you will have to pay at least 10 percent more than he or she is currently receiving. Ten percent seems to be the point at which people will jump from one company to another.

Don't be afraid to pay for talented people. Remember, you always get what you pay for, in any job market.

Start Them off Right

Good people are too valuable and scarce today for the old sink or swim method. New employees, even those with extensive previous experience, require a hands-on approach to a new job. The way you start the employee will largely determine his or her performance and effectiveness in the months and years ahead.

Start by explaining the values, vision, mission, and purpose of the company to the new employee. Explain how and why your company's products really do make a difference for your customers and your clients. Sell the new employee on the importance and value of the job and how it fits into the contribution the company makes to society.

Introduce the new employee around on the first day. Familiarize him or her with the company. Many companies offer a one- or two-week orientation program for new employees to cover all the things we have just mentioned. At the very least, spend time with the employee at the beginning so that he or she feels welcomed into a new family.

Create a buddy system for each new person. Assign another capable person to work with this person as a buddy or friend. This friend can show the new person around and answer any of his or her questions.

When you start people off right, they will be far more positive, motivated, and committed to their jobs and to the company. The first day or two, the first week or two, are really, really important in creating the proper attitudes in the mind of the new employee.

Start Them Strong

If you have made the right selection, the new person will be eager, willing, and ready to get going in the new job. At this point, start him or her off with lots of work to do. Work overload at the beginning makes the job challenging and exciting.

At the same time, provide lots of opportunity for feedback and discussion about the work. When people have ample opportunity to talk and ask questions about the job, they integrate themselves into the company much more rapidly. They are far more motivated and committed to doing a good job than if they are started off slowly or they get limited feedback.

As soon as the person begins, you should find an opportunity to catch him or her doing something right. Meet with the person, talk to her, and give her praise and encouragement at every opportunity. People are hyper-sensitive during the first days and weeks of the new job and are most open to positive influence at this time. Make sure that these are bright, shining moments for the new employee so that he or she feels really happy about working for you and with you.

Solve Problems Quickly

We are living in a world of incredible change and turbulence. Because people are complex, misunderstandings can and will frequently take place. Personality and performance problems can arise even among the very best and most capable people. Often these misunderstandings and problems are not the fault of the employee at all.

When a problem of any kind arises, deal with it quickly. Many problems are temporary and fleeting, caused by external events, and they blow over quickly. You should call the person into your office or go and see him or her immediately to deal with the difficulty, whatever it is.

Resist the temptation to blame, accuse, or pass judgment. Instead, be empathetic and supportive. Rather than accusing or demanding, ask questions to get clarity about what has happened. Listen patiently to the answers.

Remember, many employment problems are the fault of the company or the supervisor. The fact is that nobody deliberately does something that they feel is wrong. Everybody wants to do a good job and be accepted by others.

Two Common Problems

Two key problems cause most difficulties in the workplace: lack of direction and lack of feedback.

With lack of direction, the person is not exactly clear about what you want and expect. In the absence of clear, specific instructions and standards of performance, the individual will do the very best that he or she possibly can, with his or her limited knowledge and experience. The biggest single demotivator in the world of work is not knowing what's expected. On the other hand, the biggest single motivator in the world of work is being told exactly what is expected.

Lack of performance feedback is another major source of difficulties. People need to know, on a regular basis, how well they are doing. If they are making a mistake, they need this pointed out to them. If they are doing it right, they need to have this affirmed and recognized.

Fully 99 percent of problems at work are caused by miscommunication or lack of communication of some kind. The superior executive always assumes that it is he or she who is at fault when an employee fails to perform to an expected standard. When you start from that point of view, you will solve most of your performance problems quickly and easily.

Improve Performance Professionally

Job descriptions and job requirements are changing so rapidly that you must continually redefine them for each employee. Here are five simple steps that you can use on a regular basis to improve the performance of every person who reports to you.

First, sit down and explain clearly what the employee is expected to do. Describe the results that you want from the job. Make the results clear and objective. If it is important enough, write it out so that the employee can read it and take it away with him or her.

Second, set measurable standards of performance for the job you want done. Put numbers on everything. Put financial measures on every single output responsibility, if possible. One of the great rules in management is, "What gets measured gets done."

Third, never assume that the employee completely understands what you are saying. When you have delegated an assignment, ask the employee to repeat it back to you in his or her own words. Never meet with a staff member to delegate an assignment without insisting that the staff member has a pad of paper on which he or she writes as you speak.

In fully 50 percent of cases, when the employee reads back what you have just said, he or she will have misunderstood your instructions. This is the time to catch the error, not later.

Give Regular Feedback

Fourth, give regular performance feedback to tell people what they are doing well and what they can change or improve.

For people to do their very best, they need regular feedback to tell them whether they are on-track or off-track. They need to know when they are doing well and when they can do better. And the newer a person is at the job, the more regular feedback is required in order to do the job well.

Fifth, inspect what you expect. Delegation is not abdication. When you delegate a job, you assign responsibility, but you are still accountable. If the job is important, inspect the job and progress toward the goal on a regular basis. Not only does this impress upon the employee the importance of the job; it gives you an opportunity to get regular feedback and catch mistakes early in the process, when the cost can be considerably less than later on.

People love the feeling of doing their job well. They love the feeling of success and contribution. People especially love to get positive feedback and recognition for having done a good job. All this is possible when you keep focused on improving employee performance.

Assume the Best of Intentions

No matter what happens, always assume that the other person is doing the very best he can with what he has. When difficulties arise in an employee's work or in a relationship in the office, always assume the best of intentions. Always assume that people mean well. Resist the temptation to become angry or impatient.

My rule is that you should never suffer stress because of dissatisfaction with the performance or behavior of someone who reports to you. You should deal with it immediately. You should never go home with a problem that you have not confronted and dealt with in some way. Here's how you do it:

First, call the person in and discuss the problem in private, with the door closed. Never criticize or correct someone in the presence of others. Behind closed doors, explain clearly that you feel that there is a problem that should be dealt with and you want to deal with it immediately.

Second, be specific about the problem or misunderstanding. Give concrete examples of why you are concerned. The more specific you can be, the more accurate and helpful the responses can be.

Third, hear him or her out completely. Listen carefully to his or her side of the problem. The law of the situation says that for every problem concerning any two people, there is a different situation that requires different rules and decisions to deal with it. You will often find his or her side of the problem throws an entirely new light on the situation.

Set Clear Expectations

Fourth, if he or she is at fault in some way, discuss and agree on how his or her performance is to change and by how much. People cannot hit a target that they cannot see. When you point out exactly what needs to be done to resolve this challenge, people will then know exactly what they have to do to get back on top.

Fifth, monitor the agreed-upon decision and follow up. Give feedback and additional help whenever necessary. Be supportive and helpful. Sometimes a problem employee can be turned into a superstar under the right manager.

Finally, keep accurate notes and records of the discussion. If you suspect that this problem may be the tip of an iceberg that will lead to the severance of the employee, protect yourself by keeping a written record of the discussion, when and why it took place, and what solution was agreed upon. This can save you an enormous amount of trouble later.

Satisfy Their Key Needs

To hold on to good people and to keep them performing at their very best, you need to satisfy their emotional needs, just as food satisfies their nutritional needs. Each person has three major emotional needs in the world of work: dependence, independence, and interdependence.

Dependence needs refer to the need that everyone has to be part of something bigger than him- or herself. People want to belong to something bigger than themselves. People want to feel that what they are doing makes a difference in the world. People also want the security, comfort, and satisfaction of being under the umbrella of a larger authority or organization. Satisfy this dependency need by continually making people feel happy and secure that they are working with an organization that is making a difference in the world. This satisfied dependency need is a major source of loyalty and commitment.

Satisfy Their Need for Independence

Each person needs independence as well—to stand out from the crowd, to be recognized as special and important on the basis of his or her own personal qualities and accomplishments. Whenever you say or do anything that makes people feel great about themselves as individuals, you satisfy the need for independence.

The third type of need is for interdependence: to be part of a team, to work effectively and cooperatively with others. Human beings are social animals, and most people are only happy when they are working with other people in a happy, harmonious, and productive environment. The best companies and the best managers are always looking for ways to create a greater sense of harmony, happiness, and cooperation among their people. This is a chief role of management and leadership.

The key to satisfying all three needs, dependence, independence, and interdependence, is for you to listen carefully, respond appropriately, and be flexible in your dealings with each person. Needs will differ in intensity from person to person. Your job is to be sensitive to these differences and respond to them in the right way at the right time.

Practice Participatory Management

In the old paradigm, employees were grateful to have jobs. They went to work and did what was expected of them. Then they went home. Today, however, everything has changed. Today, good people want to be fully involved in their work. In fact, "being in the know" is considered one of the major sources of job satisfaction in the world of work.

There is no other way to build a powerful, positive team of highly motivated people than by bringing them together on a regular basis to talk, discuss, argue, work out problems, make plans, and generally share information, ideas, and experiences.

Hold Regular Meetings

One of my clients told me that his company had been losing money for two years and was on the verge of going broke. Then he learned about the importance of weekly meetings amongst all staff levels. When he called his managers together for the first weekly meeting, they were extremely suspicious. But after two or three weeks of open meetings, the barriers came down, and people began making suggestions to increase sales, cut costs, and improve profits.

Within six months, the entire company had turned around. Sales and profitability soared. All the managers began having weekly staff meetings as well. The psychological climate in the company went from fearful and distrustful to happy and high energy in a very short period of time.

Here is the rule. You should have staff meeting at least once each week with all the people who report to you. At this meeting, every person is on the agenda, as an agenda item. Each person is invited to report what she is doing and how it is working, to offer suggestions, and to make any requests for required resources.

You will be absolutely amazed at how effectively these open meetings build a wonderful sense of friendship and cooperation among your team. All kinds of problems get ironed out quickly. People begin to share their own personal experiences. And best of all, everyone begins to laugh together and see themselves as part of something valuable and worthwhile.

A warning: It's absolutely vital that you keep staff meetings from becoming CEO lectures. Your main job at these meetings is not to talk but to listen. Let your staff drive the topics of conversation. Staff meetings in which the staff spend interminable hours listening to the leader expound on whatever moves him or her are a waste of time for the staff and will be resented.

The more you involve your staff at every level in every decision, the more motivated and enthusiastic they will be to carry out the decisions and to achieve the successes that you desire. Participatory management is one of the most powerful of all motivational techniques in building a high performance organization.

Create a Great Place to Work

Employee retention is one of the most critical elements of business success in today's dynamic market. Once you have hired, trained, placed, and developed a team of excellent people, it is absolutely essential that you do everything possible to, as Shakespeare said, "Bind them to you with hoops of steel." The way that you create a great place to work is to, as W. Edwards Deming said, "Drive out fear."

Your job is to create a high trust environment where people feel terrific about themselves. And the way that you do this is by refusing to criticize, condemn, or complain about anything. Do not blame other people for making mistakes or for getting things wrong. Create an environment where the fears of failure and rejection that everyone carries are simply eliminated from the workplace.

Allow Honest Mistakes

The key to building a high trust environment is to allow people to make honest mistakes without criticizing them or making them feel bad or deficient in any way. When people feel that they have the permission to take risks and make mistakes without any fear of retribution, they will tend to be more thoughtful and creative in achieving the company's goals than under any other conditions.

Whenever somebody does something that doesn't work out, and this will happen often, instead of criticizing, help the person to identify the valuable lesson or lessons contained in this experience. Focus on the future rather than the past. Focus on the solution rather than the problem. When someone makes a mistake, ask, "Okay, what do we do from here? What's the next step? The next time this comes up, why don't we do it this way?"

Help People Learn and Grow

Help people to learn and to grow from temporary failures and setbacks. Encourage them to learn everything possible. Whenever possible, give them rewards and acknowledgment for having taken a risk in the first place.

There is a famous story told about Thomas J. Watson Sr., the founder of IBM, who called in a young vice president who had just spent $10 million on a research project that failed completely. When the young vice president arrived, he apologized and offered his resignation to Mr. Watson. He said, "You don't have to fire me, I'll go peacefully. I know I've made a mistake."

Thomas Watson replied, "Fire you? Why would I fire you? I've just spent $10 million on your education. Now, let's talk about your next assignment."

The only way people can learn and grow and develop judgment and wisdom is by trying things and making mistakes. Your job is to make sure that every lesson learned can be applied to making your company even more successful in the future. This is the way that you make your company a great place to work.

Continually Focus on the Person

This is perhaps the most important of all. If you focus on the people, the people will focus on the business. If you focus all of your energies on making people feel great about themselves, you will bring out their highest levels of creativity, positive energy, cooperation, commitment, and dedication to getting the job done and getting it done well.

It is said that there are never any bad soldiers under a good general. The fact is that morale does not rise in an organization. It filters down from the top. You set the tone for the people who report to you. You are the spark plug, the quarterback, and the key factor in the production of your entire company or department. As the leader, you are the one who is more responsible than anyone else when it comes to hiring and keeping the best people and then shaping them into a high-performance team that gets great results week after week and month after month.

Treat Them Like Volunteers

In today's incredibly tight job market, you should treat each person as though he or she were a volunteer. Imagine that you are running a nonprofit organization or a political campaign. Imagine that everyone who comes to work for you is a volunteer who is giving up personal time that they could quite easily spend somewhere else.

Because talented people are always in demand, each person who works for you is, in effect, a volunteer as well. Each person can go somewhere else. Each person you talk to has lots of opportunities. And the better they are, the more opportunities they have and the faster they can go somewhere else if they are not happy where they are.

When you treat each person like a volunteer and continually express your appreciation to them for working with you and helping you to achieve your goals, your attitude will be considerably different. You will always be polite and courteous. You will always be positive and encouraging. You will always be friendly and supportive. You will never criticize or complain or get angry when things go wrong. After all, you remind yourself, these people are volunteers, and they can leave at any time if they are not happy.

Respect Your Employees

In the early days and throughout their entire careers at your company, your employees must feel that you sincerely respect them. Respect is the key to keeping the best people. In the past, leaders did not respect their subordinates. They felt that employees and front-line workers were somehow inferior human beings who could not be trusted. Delegation, the sharing of information, constructive and positive feedback, and asking staff and employees for their feedback and suggestions were all out of the question. The concept that employees should be treated as volunteers would have been ridiculed by old-time managers. Employees were people to command and control. Period.

If your best people get the message that you do not truly respect them, they will go work somewhere else. If you follow the rules and advice in this chapter—if you satisfy their needs for dependence, independence, and interdependence, practice participatory management, allow for honest mistakes, help people grow and learn, and treat them as volunteers—you will find that your best will want to stay with you and your organization for as long as they can.

Hire the Best People

At every stage in the development of the economy, different skills and abilities are necessary to survive and thrive. At one time, you had to be hard-driving and focused to get the job done and outperform the competition. You had to make sure that everybody around you was the same way. Today, however, things are different. Today, the most important skill you can possibly develop is the ability to hire and keep the best people. This ability will have a greater effect on your success and happiness than any other single skill you can acquire.

It has been said that all of life is the study of attention. Where your attention goes, your life goes as well. When you begin to pay special attention to hiring and keeping great people, you will get better and better at it. You will become more and more skillful in your ability to interview and hire. You will become more and more competent in your ability to manage and motivate. You will become more and more valuable to yourself and your organization.

CHAPTER SIX

Building Winning Teams

*"A clear vision, backed by definite plans,
gives you a tremendous feeling of confidence
and personal power."*

—BRIAN TRACY

All work is done by teams. Your ability to assemble and manage a high-performance team of motivated individuals Is one of the keys to your value and effcctiveness as an executive at every stage of your career.

Team dynamics and group processes involving thousands of people have been studied extensively at a cost of millions of dollars. Today, we know more about how you can assemble a winning team than ever before.

Just as you use a recipe to prepare a dish in the kitchen, a specific recipe has been proven to work in building a high-performance, self-directed work team. When you apply this recipe—these ideas and principles—on a regular basis, until they become habitual and automatic, you will get far greater results from your people than you ever imagined possible.

Room for Improvement

As I mentioned in the previous chapter, the average employee works at only 50 percent of capacity. According to studies and observation, people spend much of their time in idle chit-chat with coworkers, surfing the Internet, going for coffee, taking long lunches, reading the newspaper, taking care of personal business, and both arriving late and leaving early.

Staff costs represent 60 to 80 percent of the total cost of operating your business. Your job is to get your highest return possible on your investment in human assets.

Today, all work is done by teams. Unless you run a shoe shine stand, you are dependant upon many other people for the quality and quantity of your work, and many other people are depending upon you.

The manager's output is the output of the team, and the output of the team is the manager's output. You do not perform alone; you perform with others.

Because of this, you must have a total commitment to peak performance from every single team member if you are going to "win games." Gaining that commitment is your responsibility.

Competence and Commitment

There are two dimensions upon which you can measure and analyze each employee: competence and commitment. These two dimensions allow you to categorize your staff into four quadrants.

Imagine a box divided into four squares. The upper-left-hand square encompasses those people who are both competent and committed. These are the *outperformers*, who accomplish 80 percent of the results—your most valuable people. These are the 20 percent of people that you build your business around.

The second quadrant, the upper right, contains people who are competent but not committed to you, your company, or the values that you stand for. They do a good job, but they do not "buy in" to your business. These employees turn out to be the major source of internal and external problems. These are the people who complain, play politics, resist your authority, and often demoralize the other people around them. Your strategy with these people is to sell them on becoming good team players, as described in the next section.

The third quadrant, the lower left, represents the people who are committed but not competent. They are nice people, but they are not excellent at their work. These people can be trained. Your goal should be to give them the training and experience necessary to move them up into the "competent and committed" quadrant.

The worst employees of all are those in the lower-right-hand quadrant, the people who are neither competent nor committed. Once you have identified these people, you must get rid of them as quickly as possible before they drag down the rest of your organization.

Four Motivation Factors

To help people become happy, productive members of the team, you must understand their motivations. People at work are most motivated by four factors.

The first is *challenging, interesting work*. Most people want to be busy and happy at work, doing things that keep them active and force them to stretch, to move out of their comfort zones, to continually learn and grow. People won't buy into the goals and objectives of a team if they are given only the most mundane tasks.

Second, people are highly motivated by working in a *high trust environment*. This is created by keeping people in the know.

When people feel that they are aware of everything that affects their work and their position, they have higher levels of trust and motivation to perform than if they feel that they are being kept in the dark.

Perhaps the best way to keep people in the know, as I have emphasized throughout this book, is to have regular weekly staff meetings, where everyone gets a chance to talk about what they are doing in front of everyone else. This is one of the most powerful team building exercises of all.

Third, people are motivated by being made *personally responsible for results*. This is one of the most powerful tools of all to build competence and confidence in people. Give them important, challenging work to do and then support them while they do that work. The more responsibility a person takes on, the more he or she grows as a decision maker and leader and the more valuable he or she will be to your company.

Fourth, people are motivated by opportunities for *personal growth and promotion*. Many people will take or stay at a job that pays less than they can earn somewhere else if they feel that they are becoming better skilled and more competent as a result of the work they do. They know inherently that these additional skills and experiences will make them more valuable in the future.

Much to the surprise of most managers, *money* and *working conditions* are fifth and sixth on the list of what motivates people at work.

The Dynamics of Top Teams

The dynamics of top teams and the reasons for their outstanding performance have been studied for many years, all over the world. The teams in these studies had all achieved remarkable business successes.

They had reduced costs dramatically in short periods of time in order to stay competitive in tough markets. They had often reduced product development time from three years to six months. Some had created brand new products and industries in the face of vigorous competition and gone on to world domination.

Each of these top teams have five characteristics in common:

1. Shared Goals

The first characteristic of top teams is that they share goals and objectives. Each team member is perfectly clear about the job to be done. They know the answer to the question, "What exactly are we trying to do?"

Top teams seem to be highly interactive. They discuss and agree on the ideal future vision of what the perfect product or service would look like or what their goal would look like if they achieved it. They discuss, explain, and agree completely on exactly what needs to be done. There is a direct relationship between the amount of time taken to discuss the goals of the team and each person's level of commitment to achieving those goals when the discussion is over.

When your team comes together, the first questions to ask are, "What results are expected of us? What are we trying to do? How are we going to go about doing it?"

The second area to be resolved is your standards of performance. How will the team measure progress, and how will they know that the job has been done well?

You can't hit a target that you can't see. If people are not clear about the results or clear about how results will be measured, the job usually does not get done. If it does get done, there are often unnecessary delays, problems, and defects.

2. Shared Values

The second quality of top teams seems to be shared values, shared beliefs, and shared principles.

Prior to beginning the team task, the members sat down and asked, "What do we stand for? What do we believe in? What are our common unifying principles? How will we govern our relationships together? On what basis?"

"Do we believe in the importance of integrity? Of being honest and open at all times with each other? Do we agree that, although we disagree, we will each show respect for each other? Will we always tell the truth? Will we resolve to accept responsibility and refuse to make excuses when things go wrong?"

Living in harmony with your innermost values and convictions is essential to feeling good about yourself and your work and to performing at your best. It is said that every human problem can be resolved with a return to values. What are yours?

3. Shared Plans

The third quality of high performing work teams is shared plans. Everyone discusses and agrees about both the goal and how that goal is to be achieved.

Socrates said, "We only learn something by dialoguing about it."

Once you are clear about goals and standards, you have to set deadlines and sub-deadlines for each task. Each person must know exactly what he or she is expected to do, and to what standard, by what time.

The best thing about group discussion is that, at the end, individual responsibility is clearly illuminated. Everybody knows exactly what they're expected to do, and they know what everyone else is expected to do, as well.

One of the biggest motivators of excellent, timely work is *peer pressure*. When everybody knows what everyone else is expected to do, a powerful, unspoken pressure not to fail in the performance of your task results. Everyone is watching and evaluating.

Shared ownership of a desired result leads to a feeling of mutual commitment and empowerment. It gives people feelings of both autonomy and dependence. It makes individuals feel proud of themselves and their personal performance and happy to be part of a larger team.

4. Clear Leadership

The fourth quality of high performance teams is that the team leader is visible. He leads the action. He is out in front.

The team leader keeps involved with each person and each task, continually offering encouragement and feedback.

Top team leaders lead by example; they set the standard. They see themselves as role models for others and always carry themselves as though everyone else was watching, even when no one is.

The best team leaders accept total responsibility for the members of the team. They go to bat for them when internal misunderstandings or difficulties arise. They stand up for them if they are criticized or attacked by other people. They are loyal to the members of their team, and the members of their team are well aware of this.

A good team leader acts as a blocker, always looking for ways to remove obstacles from the individual team members' performance. The leader runs interference and gets the team member the time, money, and resources he or she needs to get the job done.

The good team leader sees himself as a helper and as a facilitator of teamwork and team activities.

5. Continuous Evaluation and Appraisal

The fifth quality of high performance teams is continuous performance evaluation and appraisal. Most activities and projects at work encounter problems and unexpected reversals, over and over again. Mistakes are more common than successes. The best rule to adopt is that failure is merely another form of feedback.

Good teams continually ask their customers, the people who use their work, for feedback. In business, everyone has several customers. Your boss is a customer. He or she plays a huge role in your success or non-success. Your peers or colleagues, who also depend upon you to do your job, are your customers as well. You must be clear about what they want and expect from you.

As a leader, your staff are also your customers. If you do not take good care of them, you will be unable to satisfy the customers on either side of you and your boss above you.

Finally, you must be hypersensitive to your customers in the marketplace, the people who buy or don't buy your product or service. Good teams continually ask their customers how they feel about their current performance and what they could do better in the future.

Top teams also use negative feedback to improve performance. If a customer complains, they ask what they could do in the future to better please the customer in some way.

Top teams incorporate negative feedback, complaints, product or service deficiencies, and negative comparisons with competitors into their thinking and look for ways to resolve them in product design or delivery. Their motto is, "Complaints are good."

Four Stages of Team Performance

In team dynamics, there are four stages of development: forming, storming, norming, and performing.

First the team *forms.* The members come together. Everyone is happy and looking forward to the work with the team. Morale is high. Expectations of high performance are also high at this point. But little gets done.

Then reality sets in. Areas of disagreement arise. People take sides. Egos get involved. As the team begins to argue and debate over the goals and the means of attaining those goals, they move into the *storming* phase. Performance plunges. Nothing gets done.

As they get to know each other and discuss the goals and how each member can help to achieve them, they pass through the storming phase. Each person becomes comfortable with his or her role, and the team moves into the *norming* phase. Performance begins to pick up as the team starts to work more smoothly together.

Finally, the team starts to work smoothly and cohesively together, and they move into the *performing* stage. In this stage, the team starts to achieve real results.

The key to high performance work teams is harmony. In a family, harmony is the key to happy relationships. It is the same at work.

Managing Your Team

Top teams and good leaders practice what is called *management by exception.* This means that once the task has been assigned, as long as it is on schedule and on budget, no reporting is necessary. The individual only has to report back if there is an exception to the agreed-upon plan and schedule. The better and more competent your people are, the more you can practice management by exception with them.

You can also practice *management by responsibility*. Make people completely responsible for the successful completion of a particular task. Then get out of their way and leave them alone. It is amazing what people will accomplish when they feel that they are personally responsible and that they have no excuses to fall back on.

Resolve Conflict Among Team Members

Whenever there is conflict among team members, the leader brings them together and forces them to work it out one-on-one. There is no gunny-sacking and no hidden agenda. Everyone is encouraged to be straightforward and honest about their feelings and frustrations.

It is seldom possible for people to work together in a close environment without friction and disagreements. The only thing that matters is how effectively these clashes are dealt with so that they can be resolved and everyone can get on with the job. This is a responsibility of the leader.

People drop the ball. People disappoint and fail to deliver the expected results on time. Often, people will do substandard work. Peter Drucker said, "The only thing that you will always have in abundance is ordinary people. All work must be designed so that it can be done to an acceptable level of quality by ordinary people."

Qualities of Top Sports Teams

Many of the most successful sports teams have been studied over the years to learn the characteristics and qualities that enable them to prevail in highly competitive leagues against determined and aggressive competitors. Many of the principles practiced by the winning sports teams are directly applicable to building the winning business team. Synergy, teamwork, and personal empowerment are the keys to high-performance work teams. Excellent organizations are those where people feel terrific about themselves. Here are some of the characteristics of the best sports teams.

Clear Coaching and Leadership

The first noticeable characteristic of winning sports teams is clear coaching and leadership. Everyone knows that someone specific calls the plays. At work, everyone has only one boss, and everyone knows who the boss is.

In winning teams, the coach—the leader—sets high performance standards for the team. The team can never perform to higher standards than those the leader sets and enforces.

Winning teams, especially those in the best companies, expect to win, to excel, to do a good job. They take tremendous pride in the quality of their work. They continually strive to improve.

High Consideration Factor

A key part of clear coaching and leadership, in business and in sports, is a high consideration factor. The leader is continually asking people about how they think and feel, both in business and in their personal lives. The feeling that "My boss cares about me" motivates people to do their very best.

The best teams bring an intensive focus to the training and development of their people. W. Edwards Deming, the quality control expert, was once asked if training was mandatory. He replied, "Training in business is not mandatory, but neither is survival."

According to the American Society for Training and Development, the top 20 percent of profit-making companies in America spend 3 percent or more of their gross revenues on training. And they don't cut back when the economy goes soft. They consider training to be as much a necessity as advertising, promotion, or any other key business activity. Training and development show employees that the leader truly wants them to succeed—that all the talk about caring for employees is not just lip service.

Bring Out the Strengths in Each Person

The best teams focus on bringing out the strengths in each person. As Drucker said, "The purpose of an organization is to maximize strengths and to make weaknesses irrelevant."

The best teams and organizations concentrate over and over again on the basics. The vice president of a large bank told me recently, "We don't do one million transactions per day; we do one transaction over and over again one million times."

The top teams develop the talent they have rather than complaining about their people. Weak managers are always saying, "If only I had better people!"

But the job of the leader, and the team, is to elicit extraordinary performance from ordinary people, because, generally speaking, that is all you are likely to have to work with.

Planning and Strategy

The best sports teams place a heavy emphasis on planning and strategy.

They invest a lot of time, thought, and discussion into what they are doing and how they are planning to do it. They continually analyze their own performance and compare it against their competitors.

Just like winning teams, the best leaders have clear plans, goals, and objectives going into every game. The time management principle mentioned earlier says that every minute spent in planning saves 10 minutes in execution.

Selective Player Assignments

The best teams implement selective player assignments. They assign players to positions based on their potential contribution to overall team performance. They rotate a player into another position if he or she is not doing well. A rule in management says, "A weakness is often a strength inappropriately applied."

Marshall Goldsmith in his bestselling book *What Got You Here Won't Get You There* points out that many executives reach a senior position with behaviors that are no longer appropriate to their increased responsibilities. To be effective in their new positions, they often have to adapt specific elements of their personality and adjust to the requirements of the new situation.

Supportive Interaction and Open Communication

One key aspect of excellent management in sports teams is encouraging supportive interaction and open communication. The best teams practice a high level of give and take. There is plenty of feedback and discussion of performance. They have open arguments and disagreements.

In good companies, conflict resolution is achieved through confrontation and openness. Everyone knows what each other is thinking, because each person is open about thoughts, feelings, and concerns. Even in areas of disagreement, there is respect for each others' performance and contribution to the overall team or company.

Finally, top teams in both business and sports make a commitment to excellence. They do good work, win games, and are personally proud of their roles in the organization.

Each person is committed to success and profitability. They are committed to doing their jobs well and better. They believe in continuous and never-ending improvement.

Your ability to select the right people and then to organize them into a high-performance team that achieves excellent results is the true mark of great leadership.

CHAPTER SEVEN

Problem Solving and Decision Making

"People with goals succeed because they know where they are going."

—EARL NIGHTINGALE

Your entire success as a person and a leader is determined by your ability to solve problems effectively and well. Whatever title is written on your business card, your real job is problem solver. All day long, in every situation, you solve problems.

Leaders don't react to problems with anger or frustration; they look upon problems as the essential defining skill area of their work. As a leader, your job is to become extremely effective at solving any problem that is brought to you, large or small.

Fortunately, we know more about how to solve problems effectively today than we have ever known before. By practicing the approaches, skills, and techniques used by other successful leaders, you can dramatically increase your ability to solve virtually any problem that comes across your desk.

Remember, you are a knowledge worker; you work with your mind. Your productivity can only be measured by your results, by what you actually accomplish. And what stands between you and those results is always a problem or a roadblock of some kind.

The Three Qualities of Genius

In becoming better at problem solving, you can develop within yourself these three qualities of geniuses, identified through the ages.

1. The first quality of a genius, irrespective of IQ, is the ability to concentrate single-mindedly on a single goal, a single problem, or a single question without growing tired or bored.

2. The second quality of geniuses is mental flexibility. The genius refuses to rush to judgment. Instead the genius spends a lot of time considering all the various possible ways of approaching or solving the problem or answering the question.

3. The third quality of geniuses is that they use a systematic method to solve any problem. As with a mathematical formula, when you approach each problem in a systematic way and follow in a series of proven steps to walk through the problem, you dramatically increase your ability to function at higher mental levels. You will soon be astonished at the quality and quantity of ideas that you come up with.

The fact is that you are a potential genius. You can dramatically increase your inborn creativity by regularly applying these methods and techniques to problems or goals, large or small. The more often you use these methods and techniques, the smarter and more effective at problem solving you will become.

Are You Sure There Is a Problem?

When you are solving problems, be sure to avoid *blocking assumptions*. These assumptions may not be true, and they interfere with your ability to think clearly.

The first blocking assumption is that there is even a problem. Sometimes there is no problem—just facts, like the rain or the weather. For example, the market is down, or interest rates are higher. These are facts, not problems.

The second blocking assumption is that you are the person who has to solve the problem. Maybe this problem belongs in someone else's court, not yours.

The third blocking assumption is that no one has already solved the problem somewhere else. Ask, "Who else may have had this problem and come up with a solution to it?"

The fourth blocking assumption is that you have to solve the problem by some deadline. Sometimes you put unnecessary pressure on yourself. Some problems can be delayed or deferred for days, weeks, or even months.

The fifth blocking assumption is that you must completely solve the problem with a single solution. There are usually many different ways to solve a problem, including not doing anything at all.

Systematic Problem Solving Method

There is a systematic method of problem solving that is used by the most effective executives in almost every organization. It is easy to learn and apply, and it is incredibly effective in helping you overcome obstacles and achieve your goals.

First, define your problem or goal clearly in writing. Remember, a goal unachieved is merely a problem unsolved. The more clearly you define your problem or goal, the more likely it is that you will find an answer or solution.

Second, once you have defined your problem clearly, ask "What else is the problem?" Never be satisfied with a single definition of a problem. As Jack Welch said, "Continually expand your definition of the problem, and you expand your view of all the different ways that it can be solved."

Third, restate the problem to make it easier to solve. If you settle for a quick definition of the problem, it could lead you down the wrong path, to solving the wrong problem and wasting resources for no purpose.

For example, the biggest problem that a company usually experiences is low sales, leading to low revenues and decreased cash flow. When we ask, "What is the problem?" our clients will say, "Our sales are too low."

We then encourage them to expand the definition of the problem. We ask, "What else is the problem?" The answers we eventually arrive at change the entire nature of the solution and the proposed action.

What else is the problem? "Our competitor's sales are too high."

If this is truly the case, this requires changes in marketing, sales, product quality, positioning, and many other things.

What else is the problem? "We are not attracting enough qualified leads with our advertising."

If this is truly the problem, new strategies in marketing, advertising, and public relations and new choices in advertising media, copy, and advertising material are necessary.

What else is the problem? "We are not closing enough of the customers attracted by our advertising."

If this is the answer, then the solution is to train and retrain the sales force so that they are more competent at converting sales leads into actual customers.

This exercise can go on and on. Its importance is simple. If you settle on the wrong definition of the problem, you will go off in the wrong direction to solve the problem and eventually have to come back and start over.

Fourth, determine all the possible causes of the problem. Ask the brutal questions. Be prepared to accept the very worst scenario. Get your ego out of the way.

Many companies have had to admit that the "real" cause of their problem is that their products or services are not good enough in comparison with their competitors. Maybe they have to admit that there is no real market for what they're selling, or that what else is available in the market is superior or cheaper than their offerings. They may even have to admit that they made a mistake entering into this market in the first place.

Fifth, determine all the possible solutions to this problem. Then force yourself to ask, "What else is the solution?"

As the business writer Ian Mitroff says, "Beware of a problem for which there is only one solution."

Creativity, brainstorming, and flexibility—the willingness to entertain all options—are key to uncovering and discovering all possible solutions. In the next sections of this chapter, I'll explore in depth the different ways to be creative in finding solutions.

Sixth, once you have done a thorough and complete analysis of the problem and laid out all the possible causes and all the possible solutions, make a decision! Any decision is usually better than no decision at all.

Seventh, once you have made a decision, assign responsibility. Who exactly is going to carry out each part of the decision?

Eighth, set a deadline. Set a schedule for reporting on progress.

Ninth, implement the plan. "A weak solution vigorously carried out is usually better than an excellent solution weakly pursued."

Tenth, check and review later to see if the solution was successful. Did you get the expected result? Be prepared to implement your Plan B if your first solution doesn't work. Always have a backup.

Creative Thinking

Leaders must be creative thinkers if they are to succeed. Creativity will help you find the solutions to the continuous stream of problems that you face on a daily basis.

There are three major creativity triggers.

1. **Intensely desired goals**
When there is something that you want very much, that you are determined to achieve, you will enjoy a continuous stream of insights and ideas that will help you to move toward the achievement of that goal.

2. **Pressing problems**
When you can clearly define the biggest problems blocking the accomplishment of your most important goals, you will trigger solutions and answers that may surprise you—and others.

3. **Focused questions**
The best leaders continually ask questions that provoke thought and reflection and often elicit responses and ideas that would have lain dormant in the absence of the questions.

Use Mindstorming to Solve Problems

Mindstorming is one of the most powerful, creative problem solving methodologies ever developed. It is often called the Twenty Idea Method.

Start by defining your goal or problem as a question. Write this question down at the top of a blank page. For example, "How do we increase our sales by 20 percent over the next 12 months?"

Then discipline yourself to write down 20 answers to the question. You can write more than 20 answers if you like, but you must work away at it until you have at least 20 answers.

When you have 20 answers, select at least one answer on your list and take immediate action on it.

If you do this exercise on a regular basis with each goal or problem that you face, you will be astonished at the quality and quantity of answers that appear under your pen. The Twenty Idea Method is one of the most powerful ways to find creative solutions to your problems.

Lead Brainstorming Sessions

Another way to stimulate creativity is through brainstorming. This creative process requires that you work with a group. The ideal number of people in a brainstorming session is between four and seven. Fewer than four people leads to less energy, and more than seven people leads to ineffectiveness.

The ideal length of a brainstorming session is between 15 and 45 minutes. When you conduct a brainstorming session, use a stop watch. Start and stop on time. Time pressure causes ideas to pop out of the people in attendance.

Begin by defining the problem or goal clearly, in a way that demands practical answers. Instead of saying, "How can we cut costs?" say, "How can we reduce costs in this specific area by 18 percent in the next 30 days?"

Make the brainstorming process *fun*. Make it a game, a race against time. Tell everyone that your goal is to get as many ideas as possible in the period of time allotted.

The key to brainstorming is to make sure that there is no judgment or evaluation of any ideas. Don't let anyone comment on the ideas as they emerge or ridicule what may seem like silly ideas. As the leader of the brainstorming session, make sure that nothing is considered out of bounds or rejected outright.

When I do strategic planning or brainstorming with my clients, I will often take out a $100 bill and hold it up before we begin. I will then say, "This $100 bill goes to the first person who asks a dumb question or makes a dumb suggestion. And I can promise you this; no one in this room is going to win this money today."

Usually, everyone laughs, and then the ideas start pouring like a river. Often, an idea that seems ridiculous or silly, when combined with another idea that seems to have no potential, creates a third idea that is the breakthrough that leads to the solution to the problem.

Recently, in a brainstorming session with a room full of professionals, I had the groups of five or six people at each table brainstorm solutions to a particular problem. After 15 minutes, they were instructed to take their written solutions to another table and trade. In the next 45 minutes, each group evaluated and discussed the ideas generated by the group at the next table. Because of this dynamic, there was no ego involved, and some of the solutions they came up with were remarkable.

Complete the Sentence

Another creativity exercise you can use to stimulate creativity in yourself and in the people who report to you is the sentence completion exercise.

The way you use this method is simple. Find as many ways as possible to finish a particular sentence. For example:

1. "We could double our sales if . . ." Then think of as many ways to complete that sentence as possible.

2. "We could cut our costs in this area by 30 percent if only . . ." Then complete the sentence with every idea you can think of to achieve this goal.

3. "We could sell more of our products or services if our customers just didn't say . . ." Identify all the objections that a qualified prospect would give *not* to buy your product or service, and think of ways of overcoming that objection.

4. "We could be the best in our business if we . . ." What are the specific steps that you could take, starting today, to improve the quality of your products and services?

Practice Zero-Based Thinking

One of the best tools for stimulating creativity is zero-based thinking, which we discussed in earlier chapters of the book. Zero-based thinking frees your mind from both conscious and unconscious limitations.

When you ask, "Knowing what I now know, is there anything that I am doing that I would *not* get into again today if I had to do it over?" your mind becomes free to observe everything you are doing more calmly and objectively.

The key to zero-based thinking is the practice of *creative abandonment.* What should you discontinue, reduce, or eliminate altogether?

Creativity in Small Steps

There is a direct relationship between the quantity of new ideas that you brainstorm and the quality of the ideas that you eventually settle upon. One new idea or insight can transform a situation, and even change your career.

The very best definition of creativity is simple improvement. The fact is that anytime you find a way to accomplish a task, or achieve results, faster, better, cheaper, or easier than before, you are exercising your creativity at a high level.

Everyone can see opportunities for improvement in their line of sight. As Theodore Roosevelt said, "Do what you can with what you have, where you are." In business, this is the zone where you will see the most opportunities for improvement.

In what ways could you improve the way you do your job, right now? How could you achieve your goals faster, better, cheaper, and easier by revising your working methods?

The Japanese developed the famous Kaizan Principle after World War II and used it to achieve some of the highest levels of quality, efficiency, and profitability in the world.

Kaizan means "continuous betterment." It is based on the law of incremental improvement. This law requires that you continuously seek out little ways to improve the quality of your products and services over time. The accumulative effect of hundreds, even thousands, of tiny improvements leads to the production of world-quality products and services.

Every day, you should be looking for ways to increase revenues, improve operations, reduce costs, and boost profits. Sometimes a single idea could save your business or transform your business into a world leader in cost effectiveness and profitability.

You Could Be Wrong

When you are developing your creative thinking skills, one of the most important things to do is test your assumptions. As I discussed in Chapter Three, your assumptions could be wrong. "False assumptions lie at the root of every failure."

Each person believes certain basic premises. Most of their thoughts, feelings, and decisions arise from a fixed view of the way the world is and the way things *should* be. But very often, these basic premises are false. They may even have resulted from accepting wrong information as true and adopting it without question. This can be very dangerous to good thinking.

In testing your assumptions, be willing to admit that you could be wrong. I encourage people, even when they feel strongly, to precede their remarks by saying, "You know, I could be wrong; I often am."

When you are willing to admit that you could be wrong, you relax, and your mind opens up to a wider range of possibilities.

Be willing to change your mind. It is amazing how people's egos get involved in their thoughts, feelings, and activities in business. They take a position and, even if it turns out to be a poor position, they do not want to change their minds because they're afraid that they will be seen as weak.

But nothing could be further from the truth. The mark of strong leaders, leaders of courage and character, is that they are willing to admit that they are wrong when it becomes clear that they are. They are not defensive. They are willing to abandon their old ideas and accept a better idea from someone else.

This is why humility is such a key quality of the great leader. Leaders who think they know everything are blinded by their egos. They cannot see what they are doing wrong, because they believe they can do no wrong.

Strong people are willing to change their minds when they get new information.

What Is the Problem?

Release your creativity and solve problems more effectively by applying the principle of constraints to your work. The principle of constraints will help you pinpoint your most damaging problems.

> **Step One**: Determine where you are today—your starting point in relation to any goal or objective you have.

> **Step Two**: Determine your goal or objective clearly. Decide exactly what you want to accomplish or where you want to be sometime in the future.

> **Step Three**: Identify the bottleneck or limiting factor between you and your goal.

> **Step Four**: Ask, "What determines the speed at which I get from where I am now to my goal in the future? What is holding me back?"

There is always one factor that, more than anything else, holds you back or determines the speed at which you achieve your goal. Sometimes we call this the *bottleneck*, or the *choke point*.

Apply the 80/20 rule to constraints. Fully 80 percent of the reasons that you are not achieving your goal at the speed you desire are contained within yourself or within your business. Only 20 percent are on the outside. Always begin by looking within to determine what is holding you back.

Once you have determined the true bottleneck, concentrate all of your energies, like a laser beam, on solving that one problem or alleviating that one constraint.

Making the Best Decision

Everything that happens in our world happens as a result of a decision or a series of decisions. As it happens, fully 70 percent of the decisions that you make ultimately turn out to be wrong!

This can be because you make your decisions on the basis of false premises, or else the situation changes completely and what appeared to be a good decision at one time turns out to be a poor decision later on.

Your ability to make timely and accurate decisions in every part of your life is the true measure of your wisdom and experience.

Good decisions lead to the proper allocation of resources, money, and people. You decide whom you are going to hire, promote, and assign to new tasks. You use decision making to solve the major and minor problems that arise all day long.

You rise to the level of your own ability to solve problems and make good decisions.

Three Stages of Business Decision Making

The basic decision making process in business goes through three stages.

First, begin with free and open discussion; consider all ideas and viewpoints.

Second, make a clear decision. Everyone agrees on what will be done, who will do it, when it will be done, and how it will be done.

The third phase in decision making is full support; everybody agrees to back the decision totally.

Four Types of Decisions

First is the decision that must be made. It cannot be put off or delegated to someone else.

Second are decisions that you do not have to make. The rule

is that if you do not have to make a decision, you have to *not* make that decision.

Third are decisions that you cannot afford to make. If the decision is wrong, the cost will be too high; you may not be able to recover.

Fourth are decisions that you cannot afford not to make. These are decisions with a very low downside if you are wrong and an enormous and positive upside if you are correct.

Two Decision Making Techniques

There are two decision making methods you can use to improve your decision making ability.

The Balance Sheet Method. This is often called the *Ben Franklin Method*. Take a sheet of paper and draw a line down the center. On one side, write all of the reasons in favor of the decision. On the other side of the line, list all of the opposing reasons. This method, pioneered by Ben Franklin, led him to become the first millionaire in America and one of the richest men in the colonies.

The Point Scoring System. Write out all of the decision criteria. List everything that you would like to accomplish with this particular decision—all of the factors that are important to you. (This is especially useful when hiring someone.)

Take a thousand points and allocate these points across all the decision criteria that you have written down. Assign a larger number of points to some factors and a smaller number to others.

This exercise helps you to become clear about which factors in the decision are most important. Since no decision is perfect, you will make the decision that earns the highest possible score, based on how you have allocated these points.

Decisiveness is the key quality for successful decision making. Any decision is better than no decision, especially if the issue is not major.

When you make a decision, be prepared to accept feedback and to self-correct. You may not necessarily make the right decisions all the time, but you can resolve to make your decisions *right.*

Discussion and Commitment

In decision making there is a direct relationship between the amount of discussion that precedes the decision and the level of commitment among the participants involved in the discussion.

Discussion is extremely important in business. Some people only understand a problem or a situation by dialoguing about it with others.

The Disaster Report

Analyze the possible adverse consequences of a decision before you make it:

1. Ask, "What is the worst possible outcome of this decision?"

2. Then fill out the "disaster report" before you finalize your decision.

3. Can you accept the worst possible outcome, should it occur?

4. If you cannot accept the worst possible negative outcome, then don't do it at all.

5. If your answer is "Yes, I can afford the worst possible outcome," then ask, "What can I do to make sure that the worst doesn't occur?"

Set Standards for Success

How will you measure if the decision was right?

1. Set clear, measurable standards and goals for every decision.

2. Monitor, review, and check in regularly to see how it is going.

3. Be prepared to change or revise your decision if you get new information.

4. Accept feedback and self-correct.

5. Be prepared to fall back on your Plan B if your original decision doesn't work.

Help Your Staff Make Decisions

Help your staff become more capable of solving problems and making decisions. Delegate both problem solving and decision making to them. Issue these instructions:

1. Before you come to me with a problem, define it clearly in writing.

2. Write down all the reasons why the problem has occurred.

3. Identify all the possible solutions to the problem. Select the solution that you think is best.

When an employee brings you a problem always ask, *"What do you think we should do?"*

Helping and allowing people to make decisions makes them stronger, smarter, and more competent. It also frees up a lot of your time, which you can put to better use elsewhere.

Learn From Every Situation

Aristotle wrote, "Wisdom is an equal combination of experience plus reflection."

Ask two questions after every experience to be sure that you extract the greatest amount of wisdom in learning possible from the experience:

1. **"What did I do right?"** Analyze everything that you did right in that particular decision, even if the decision turned out poorly. Look for the good points in your decision making process.

2. **"What would I do differently?"** Make a list of everything that you would do to make a better decision next time.

The value in these two questions is that they both demand positive answers. Instead of thinking, "What did I do wrong?" instead ask, "What did I do right?" and "What would I do differently?" This keeps your mind positive and focused on the solution and focused on the future.

The best managers in the real world are decisive. They make decisions, and then they move ahead to implement those decisions. Average managers avoid making decisions. They are too afraid of making a mistake.

Developing the quality of decisiveness, in combination with your problem solving ability, is the key to performing at your very best.

8

Communicate with Power

"A winner is someone who recognizes his God-given talents, works his tail off to develop them into skills, and uses those skills to accomplish his goals."

—LARRY BIRD

Fully 85 percent of your success as a leader will be determined by your ability to communicate effectively with others. Everything you accomplish will be associated with other people in some way. And the people in your life will account for 85 percent of your happiness and your success.

The quality of your communications, therefore, determines the quality of your life and the quality of your relationships, of all kinds.

The good news is that communicating is a skill that you can learn with practice.

In your interactions with others, there are five goals that you want to accomplish.

1. You want people to like and respect you, which will reinforce and validate your self-image but also

encourage others to want to hear you, not shut you out.

2. You want people to recognize that you are valuable and important, reinforcing your self-esteem but also giving others a reason to listen to you.

3. You want to be able to persuade people to accept your point of view, to sell your products, services, and ideas to others.

4. You want to get people to change their minds and to cooperate with you in achieving your goals.

5. Overall, you want to be more personally powerful and influential in all your relationships, personal and business.

These are the keys to success in leadership, life, and love.

Aristotle's Rhetoric: The Three Parts of Any Communication

According to Aristotle, each conversation or discourse is made up of three elements.

1. **Ethos:** The character of the person speaking.

2. **Pathos:** The emotions that you address in your audience.

3. **Logos:** The words you use (least important!).

The most effective communication addresses all three of these elements. First, the person speaking has the credibility and respect required to be heard. Second, the communication methods take into careful account the emotions of the listeners. Third, the message itself, whether conveyed through casual conversation, a formal speech, or any other type of presentation, is well researched, structured, and delivered.

Four Keys to Persuasion

There are four keys to persuasion that you can develop and use to persuade others more effectively. They are called the *Four Ps*.

1. **Positioning.** Your personal credibility: How people think and talk about you—your reputation amongst the people you are trying to persuade

2. **Performance.** Your ability and competence in your field; having a reputation for expertise and knowledge

3. **Personal Power.** Your power or control over people, money, or resources

4. **Politeness.** Your use of kindness, courtesy, and respect in your dealings with other people

In the traditional command-and-control culture of organizations, personal power was perhaps the most important key to persuasion. When the boss spoke, people listened. While power is still an important factor in whether people will listen to you, we know now that ordering somebody to buy into a message is not a sustainable way to persuade people. If they don't believe in what you want them to do, they will not do it well, even if they have to do it because "you're the boss."

With regard to the fourth *P*, one of the most powerful influence factors in human relationships is liking. The more that people like you, the more open they are to being persuaded and influenced by you. This is a key to effective communication.

But you must also be credible and competent. People may like you but still not be sure that you have the experience, knowledge, or information to support what you are saying.

The most important word in persuasion, influence, and communicating with power is credibility. The key question is, "How much does the person like you, trust you, and believe in what you say?"

The rule is: Everything counts! Everything helps or hurts. Everything you do or say adds up or takes away from your credibility. Nothing is overlooked or ignored.

Concentrate on developing a reputation for honesty and dependability. People will buy more and pay more from a person or company that has high credibility than from one that offers a better, cheaper product or service but is not reliable.

Look the Part

Credibility can be harmed or helped to a surprising degree by how you look. To communicate effectively with others, you must look the part. People are 95 percent visual in their thinking about you.

1. It takes only *four* seconds to make the first impression.

2. It takes only 30 seconds to finalize the person's initial impression of you.

3. After the first impression has solidified, people seek reasons to justify and validate the impression they have already made. Simultaneously, they reject information that contradicts that impression.

4. Dress for success! Your clothes create as much as 95 percent of your first impression to others, because they cover 95 percent of your body.

    a) Buy and read books and articles on how to dress powerfully and persuasively in every situation.

    b) Look at the most successful and respected people around you, and notice how they dress.

    c) Make them your role models; copy their ways of dress and grooming.

Preparation Is the Mark of the Professional

If you look the part, you have passed the first test of credibility. But if you look good but are apparently unprepared or confused, your newfound credibility will disappear. Prepare thoroughly for every important meeting with others, especially in business. Do your homework before every meeting. Remember:

> People know immediately when you are well prepared for a meeting. When you are, your credibility goes straight up.

> People know immediately when you are unprepared for a meeting; your credibility goes straight down.

Your Emotional Intelligence

In 1995, Daniel Goleman wrote the book *Emotional Intelligence*. He argued that EQ is more important than IQ.

He concluded that your ability to persuade others is the highest form of emotional intelligence and the true measure of how effective you are as a person.

The question is this: How do you get your ideas across to others, get people to cooperate with you, and develop the abilities to communicate, influence, and persuade others?

People do things for their reasons, not yours. Motivation requires *motive*. To communicate and persuade effectively, you must find out what their motives really are.

The key is to get out of yourself and enter into the mind, heart, and situation of the other person. Focus on the needs and desires of the other person rather than your own.

Your Persuasive Abilities

You can only persuade and influence others if they believe that you can do something for them or to them, or if they believe that you can stop something being done to or for them.

People are motivated by two major factors:

Desire for gain: physical, material, financial, and emotional;

Fear of loss: physical, material, financial, and emotional.

The fear of loss is two and a half times more powerful than the desire for gain in motivating human behavior. If you offer a person a dollar, their desire for gain is 1.0 in strength. But if you threaten to take a dollar away, their fear of loss is 2.5 in strength. This is why the threat of loss of any kind can often trigger such strong emotions.

Everything is perception: Whether people perceive you as

being able to help them or hurt them in some way determines your ability to influence or persuade them to do what you want.

Most of human behavior is based on the *expediency factor*. This is the natural tendency of most people to act expediently most of the time.

The expediency factor is defined this way: People always strive to get the things they want the fastest and easiest way possible, with little immediate concern for the long-term consequences of their behaviors.

Your job in persuasion is to make your idea or proposal appear to be the most expedient way for the other person to achieve his personal and business goals.

Make Them Feel Important

The deepest need in human nature is to feel valuable and important. You trigger this feeling by doing everything possible to raise the person's self-esteem, to help them to like themselves even more.

You should imagine that every person in your company is wearing a sign around his or her neck, all day long, that says, "Make me feel important." In every interaction with every single person, you should respond to this basic human request. You should always be looking for ways to make people feel important and valuable as parts of your team.

Practice the Four A's Daily

There are four key behaviors that you can practice every day to make people feel important. They all begin with the letter *A*.

1. Appreciation. Take every opportunity to thank each person for everything that he or she does, small or large, in the process of carrying out their duties.

Every time you say "Thank you" to a person, his or her self-esteem goes up. He or she feels better and more valuable. And he or she is even more motivated to do more of the things for which they received appreciation in the first place. A boss with an "Attitude of gratitude" is one of the most effective leaders in any organization.

2. **Approval**. The second way to make people feel valuable is to express approval. Give praise and approval on every occasion for every accomplishment of whatever size. Give praise for every good effort. Give praise for every good suggestion or idea. Especially, praise people when they do something that goes above and beyond the call of duty. Praise immediately, praise specifically, and praise regularly.

Whenever you praise people, they experience it physically and emotionally. Their self-esteem rises, and they feel happy inside. And whatever you praise gets repeated. In fact, the definition of self-esteem is "the degree to which a person feels himself or herself to be praiseworthy."

3. **Admiration.** The third self-esteem building behavior you can practice is admiration. As Abraham Lincoln said, "Everybody likes a compliment." Continually compliment people on their traits, such as punctuality and persistence. Compliment them on their possessions, such as their clothes, cars, and accessories. Compliment them on their accomplishments, both at work and in their private lives.

Every time you admire something about another person, you raise that person's self-esteem and make them feel happier and more committed to you and the company.

4. Attention. The fourth behavior, perhaps the most important of all, is the behavior of attention. This simply means that you listen to your staff, and to members of your family, when they want to talk to you. Listen patiently. Listen quietly. Listen calmly. Listen thoughtfully. Listen without interrupting.

Remember, you do not have to act on the ideas or suggestions of people who talk to you. You just have to listen carefully, nod, smile, and thank them for their input. People get tremendous satisfaction from having an opportunity to express themselves honestly to their bosses, and to other important people in their lives. Of course, if you are listening carefully, you are also thinking about what people are saying, and you may decide that their ideas or suggestions require action. Don't just go through the motions. True listeners hear what's being said to them.

Leaders are listeners. Effective listening is the key to leadership, persuasion, and good communications. It is so powerful that it is sometimes called *White Magic.*

Four Keys to Being a Great Listener

1. Listen attentively. Lean forward. Don't interrupt. When you listen attentively, you raise the other person's self-esteem and make him or her feel important.

2. Pause before replying. This benefits you in three ways:

    a) You avoid the risk of interrupting if the speaker is just pausing to reorganize his or her thoughts.

    b) Pausing allows you to hear at a deeper level and understand more of what the speaker really means.

    c) Your silence makes it clear that you are carefully considering what the other person has said, making him or her feel more important.

3. Question for clarification. Never assume that you know what the other person meant by what he or she just said. Instead, ask:

"How do you mean?" or "How do you mean, exactly?"

"And *then* what did you do?"

"How did you *feel* about that?"

Rule: The person who asks questions has control over the person who is answering the questions.

4. Feed it back; paraphrase it in your own words. This is the "acid test" of listening.

Be Sincere

Communicators are aware of the emotional element in effective communication—the importance of understanding the emotional motivations of the people with whom you're communicating. But any efforts to address emotional issues must be based in sincerity. People will know when you are saying empty words, when your appreciation, approval, admiration, or attention is completely false. Pathos is linked to ethos; emotional responses are linked to credibility. If you don't believe what you're saying, don't expect others to believe you.

According to Albert Mehrabian of UCLA, a conversation contains three elements.

1. Body language—55 percent of the message.

2. Tone of voice—38 percent of the message.

3. The words themselves—only 7 percent of the message!

If you are faking sincerity, your body language and tone of voice will probably give you away, no matter what your words say.

The Words You Use: Three Communication Tools for Success

1. The one-on-one conversation: asking questions, listening, and presenting your ideas

2. The group presentation: requires thorough preparation and good presentation skills

3. The written letter or report: can make you or break you in business situations

Good news? Each of these is a skill that is learnable by practice and repetition.

Five Keys to An Effective Presentation

There are five keys to an effective presentation:

1. Prepare thoroughly in advance; effective presentation is 90 percent preparation.

2. Present your point of view; state your idea or goal clearly at the beginning of your presentation.

3. Give the reasons you have for your point of view.

4. Give evidence for your reasons.

5. Restate your point of view once more and call for action.

The Traditional Speech Outline

Many books have been written about how to effectively give speeches. The core structure of every speech, however, is a simple three-point outline:

1. Tell them what you are going to tell them.

2. Tell them your message.

3. Tell them what you just told them, summarize your key points, and ask for action.

Remember the Expediency Principle

To influence people in business, always refer back to the expediency principle. Especially in business, people buy or decline to buy based on their conclusion that your offering is the fastest and best way to get what they want, right now—or not! Here are some tips to selling the expediency of what you are offering.

1. Present social proof. Refer to others who have bought your product or accepted your idea and are happy with it. Offer letters, lists, names, and photographs of satisfied customers.

2. Build buying desire and increase your ability to persuade by focusing on the benefits and by

answering the customer question, "What's in it for me?"

    a) Explain how the person will be better off using your product or service or accepting your idea.

    b) Imply *scarcity*. You can often increase buying desire by suggesting that there is a limited quantity or a limited quantity at that price.

    c) Use the contrast principle. Contrast the price of your item with a similar item that is substantially more expensive. This puts your price into perspective and often makes the sale.

3. Ask them to buy your product or service; don't wait for them to offer.

4. Promise them superb quality and excellent follow-up service.

If you can't communicate, you can't lead. If you can't get people to listen, you can't create followers. Resolve today to become an expert in communicating with power. Read books on the subject. Attend courses on effective communications. Most of all, practice, practice, practice!

9

The Leader's Questionnaire

"The only limit to our realization of tomorrow will be our doubts of today. Let us move forward with strong and active faith."

—FRANKLIN DELANO ROOSEVELT

The best leaders are those who have a complete and intimate understanding of every facet of their business and industry. Leaders know everything about their own companies (its strengths and weaknesses, for example), their customers, their competition, and the business environment in which they operate.

This chapter features a complete leader's questionnaire that covers all the major strategic and management issues that leaders will need to address. Some of the questions will be familiar; many will not.

Every leader should be able to answer these questions with confidence, without hesitation. If you do not know the answers, or if you are unsure, it is important that you find out as soon as possible. Without the answers to these questions, or with the wrong answers, you will make mistakes in marketing, sales, and business strategy that can be fatal to your business.

Once you've answered the questions, review your answers with the leadership staff and the other personnel in your business, who will be in the best position to confirm the truth of your answers. Be sure that you all agree.

After each question, you will find an explanation of the context of that question: why that question is important to the success of your company. In some cases, the explanation will include additional questions that will help you think not only about what is, but what could be or should be.

As Larry Bossidy writes, "Only a leader can ask the tough questions that everyone needs to answer, then manage the process of debating the information and making the right trade-offs. And only the leader who's intimately engaged in the business can know enough to have the comprehensive view and ask the tough, incisive questions."

Here are the tough questions that you and the team you lead will need to answer.

1. What business are you really in? What does your company actually *do* for your customer to improve his or her life or work?

   1. _____

   2. _____

   3. _____

Customers do not buy products or services; they buy *improvement*. They buy what you sell in anticipation of being better off in some way in the future. If this expected improvement is unclear or undesired, customers refrain from buying, or buy from someone else.

2. What is the *mission* of your company or firm? Your mission should be stated in terms of what you want to achieve, avoid, or preserve for your customers.

1. Achieve? _____

2. Avoid? _____

3. Preserve? _____

A mission is something that can be clearly defined and can be accomplished. It contains both a measure and a method. It is always defined in terms of your customer. And the simpler it is, the easier it is for your people to understand it and get behind it. AT&T's mission was "to install a telephone in every home and office in America."

3. How do your customers talk about your company, think about your company, or describe your company to others? What *words* do they use?

1. _____

2. _____

3. _____

This is referred to as your *positioning* in the hearts and minds of your existing and prospective customers. The words that people use when they think about your company, and your products and services, largely determine whether they buy or not. The choice of these words cannot be left to chance. If you are not satisfied with the current answer to this question—with the words that customers are using today—then ask yourself what words you would want them to use. What could you do to create this new perception?

4. Who is your *perfect customer*? Describe him or her demographically, in terms of age, income, education, occupation, location, and whichever other factors are appropriate for your industry.

    1. Age? _____

    2. Income? _____

    3. Occupation? _____

    4. Education? _____

    5. Needs or problems? _____

    6. Family? _____

    7. Other factors? _____

5. Describe your perfect customer *psychographically*. How does he or she think and feel in relation to buying what you sell?

    1. Desires? _____

    2. Fears? _____

    3. Hopes? _____

    4. Attitudes? _____

    5. Expectations? _____

    6. Objections? _____

THE LEADER'S QUESTIONNAIRE

6. What does your perfect customer consider of *value*? What benefits does your customer seek or expect in dealing with you?

   1. _____

   2. _____

   3. _____

Customers only buy when they feel that the benefits or rewards of buying your product will be greater than those they would receive if they bought from your competitor.

7. What are your company's *core competencies*? What special skills or abilities does your company possess that enable you to fulfill the needs of your customer?

   1. _____

   2. _____

   3. _____

A core competency is something that you do that enables you or your company to produce and sell a product in a competitive market. It is a skill or ability that you already have or that you can either hire from the outside or develop internally.

8. What does your company do extremely well? In what areas do you perform in an exceptional fashion? What makes you *superior* to your competitors?

   1. _____

2. _____

3. _____

To succeed in tough markets, you must be superior in at least three ways, such as higher quality, better or faster customer service, greater ease of use, or some other factor. What are yours? What could they be?

9. Who are your *competitors*? Who else sells your same product or service to your prospective customers?

   1. _____

   2. _____

   3. _____

The actions and decisions of your competitors determine how much you can charge, how much you sell, how much you earn, your rate of growth, and the future of your business. You should know and understand them and what they are doing at all times.

10. Who are your *biggest or main* competitors?

   1. _____

   2. _____

   3. _____

If these competitors were removed from the market, your sales would jump. What could you do to neutralize their strengths? How could you exploit their vulnerabilities? How could you make your products and services so desirable that your competitors would be unable to compete with you?

11. Who are your *secondary* competitors? Who else offers an alternative to what you sell?

    1. _____

    2. _____

    3. _____

The customer always has three choices: He can buy from you, buy from someone else, or buy nothing at all. What else could your customer buy with the same dollars that you want him to spend with you?

12. *Why* do your customers buy from your competitors? What benefits do they receive from your competitors that they don't receive from you?

    1. _____

    2. _____

    3. _____

Perception is everything. What do your customers see in your competitor's offerings that they don't perceive in yours? Why do they feel that your competitor is better than you? What could you do to offset this perception?

13. Which of your products or services give you your *highest profits*? Where do you get your highest

pay-off? What do you do in your business that gives you your highest return on effort or investment?

1. _____

2. _____

3. _____

14. Which of your products, services, markets, customers, or activities are the *least profitable*?

    1. _____

    2. _____

    3. _____

Just as a reptile sheds its skin each season, you should shed all those products and activities that may have been a good idea at the time but are no longer as profitable today as they were in the past. As a leader, you play a key role in identifying which products your company should **abandon, eliminate, or get out of,** to free up more time for higher value, more profitable activities.

15. Why do your *competitor's customers* buy from them and not from you?

    1. _____

    2. _____

    3. _____

To survive and thrive today, you are going to have to take business and customer dollars away from someone else. To attract your competitor's customers, you must first understand their motivations. Then you can lead your team in making your offerings so desirable that a demanding customer would prefer to buy from you rather than from his existing supplier.

16. Which *marketing methods* have been successful, and which have been less successful, in generating leads and attracting potential customers?

    1. _____
    2. _____
    3. _____

There is a direct relationship between the number of prospective customers your company can attract and the number of sales you will make. As the leader, you must ensure that lead generation is a central focus of all your marketing and sales activities. Understanding what works and what doesn't will also help you lead the effort to improve your company's marketing methods in order to generate more leads and attract more potential customers. Marketing is everyone's business—from the corner office to the front lines.

17. How much do you *charge?* Is this price reasonable, competitive, and profitable in today's market, based on current market conditions?

    1. _____
    2. _____
    3. _____

There are seven different elements that determine all sales and marketing success. This is called the *marketing mix*. In addition to price, the elements of the marketing mix are product (see question 1), promotion (see question 20), place (see question 18), positioning (see question 3), packaging (see question 19), and people (see question 20).

18. *Where* exactly do you sell your products and services? Are there other places that you could offer your products or services for sale?

   1. _____

   2. _____

   3. _____

19. How does your product or service look on the outside? Is there any way that you could change the way your product or service is *packaged* so that it appears more attractive and desirable to more of your ideal customers?

   1. _____

   2. _____

   3. _____

20. *Who* is going to carry out each part of your marketing and sales strategy? Do your people present the ideal image of your company and your products and services? Is there anyone working with you or for you today that, knowing what you now know, you wouldn't hire again?

   1. _____

2. _____

3. _____

21. What is your company's area of *specialization*?
What are your products or services uniquely
suited to do, and for whom?

1. _____

2. _____

3. _____

Your company can specialize in three areas. First, you can
specialize in serving a particular type of customer, being a one-
stop supply source for that customer. Second, you can specialize
in a particular product line, carrying everything that a customer
would need in that area. Third, you can specialize geographically,
offering your products and services throughout that area.

22. What is your area of *differentiation* or excellence?
In what ways are you superior to your
competitors?

1. _____

2. _____

3. _____

The essence of all advertising and marketing is differentiation: clearly pointing out why and how your product or service is
superior. Customers only buy what they perceive to be the best
choice at that moment.

23. What is your specific *competitive advantage*? What qualities of your products, services, or business make you better than 90 percent of businesses in your industry?

    1. _____

    2. _____

    3. _____

A competitive advantage is something that your competitors do not offer and that is of value to your customer. It is the key to the success of your business.

What is your competitive advantage today? What will it be in the future? What should it be if you want to increase your sales? What could it be if you wanted to dominate your market? As Jack Welch said, "If you don't have competitive advantage, don't compete."

24. What *type of customers* benefit the most from the superior benefits offered by your product or service? What type of customers most appreciate what you provide in an excellent fashion and are willing to pay for them?

    1. _____

    2. _____

    3. _____

By identifying your areas of specialization and differentiation, you clearly define those buyers who are your best prospective customers—and those who are not. You can then better slice and dice your market, allocating your scarce marketing resources to those forms of promotion where superior results are possible.

25. In what areas of advertising, promoting, and selling should you *concentrate your energy* and resources to maximize your sales and profits?

    1. _____

    2. _____

    3. _____

If you understand what works best in advertising, promoting, and selling, you will know where to concentrate your marketing energy and resources to maximize your sales and profits. One of the simplest marketing strategies is to carefully study the advertising media used by your competitors to sell to the same customers that you want to attract. If an ad runs repeatedly in a particular media, phrased in a particular way, this is a good indicator that the ad is drawing attention and paying off for the advertiser.

26. How many prospects does your sales team convert into paying customers, and what are the main factors contributing to the *conversion rates* in your company?

    1. _____

    2. _____

    3. _____

The first priority of business is to attract interested prospects. The second is to convert them into customers, into buying from you rather than from someone else. Your sales strategies and techniques in this area can make you or break you. As a leader, you must guide and enable a continued effort to increase conversion rates. How can your company convert more prospects into paying customers? The answer begins with a leadership that understands why prospects buy and why they don't. Leaders must also recognize that the market is continually changing, which means that sales strategies and techniques may also need to adapt.

27. Which *customers* are no longer worth the time and energy they take to satisfy?

    1. _____

    2. _____

    3. _____

Your bottom 20 percent of customers, because of the small quantities they buy, the amount of time it takes to service them, and the problems you have getting payment from them, should be dropped from your lists and encouraged to do business with someone else. Answering this question will help you phase out or abandon those customers, freeing up time and energy to develop even better customers.

28. What *activities* offer low or no return on your investments of time and energy?

    1. _____

    2. _____

    3. _____

You must restructure your business continually, regularly moving people and resources into the top 20 percent of the revenue-generating activities in your business. This question will help you identify which activities your company should abandon or de-emphasize to make more time for those activities that offer the highest possible return.

29. What is your *brand* in your market today? What are you known for in your market?

    1. _____   _____

    2. _____

    3. _____

Every company and product has a brand image, developed by design or created in the minds of your customers by chance. A good brand represents a value that the customer can be assured of receiving if he buys a product with that brand on it.

30. What *should* your brand be? What words or description would you like to own in your customer's mind? What kind of a reputation would be most helpful for you to develop?

    1. _____

    2. _____

    3. _____

The best definition of a good brand is "the promises you make and the promises you keep." What promises do you make to your customer when he buys your product? Do you keep these promises? Whenever you get a customer complaint, it is because the customer feels that you did not deliver on your promises.

31. How is *technology* affecting your business? In what three ways is the Internet changing the way you do business?

    1. _____

    2. _____

    3. _____

Continually seek out and explore new technologies to make your business more efficient and new Internet strategies to expand your markets.

32. What could you *change or improve* about your products, services, or overall business to begin creating a more favorable brand-image in your customers' minds?

    1. _____

    2. _____

    3. _____

Think of three things you could do immediately to make your customers happier that they dealt with you rather than someone else.

33. *Imagine* that five years from today, your company had the best name and reputation of any company in your industry. Imagine that a writer from a major magazine or newspaper was going to write a news story about you and your company. What would you want the story to say?

    1. _____

2. _____

3. _____

34. If your company was ideal in every way, how would the reporter describe the *quality* of your products and services in comparison with your competitors? What kind of reputation would you have? What words would he use?

    1. _____

    2. _____

    3. _____

35. How would the reporter describe *your business?* How would she describe you, your products, your quality of customer service, your people, and your internal operations?

    1. _____

    2. _____

    3. _____

36. If your business was perfect, what would your *annual revenues* be ? What would your *level of profitability* be? What percentage of sales? What amount in dollars?

    1. _____

    2. _____

    3. _____

37. If your company was perfect, what kind of *people* would you have working for you? What kind of managers would you have? What kind of staff? What kind of salespeople?

    1. _____

    2. _____

    3. _____

38. If your future was perfect, what would your *personal situation* be? How much would you be earning? What would your position be? Where would you be in your field and your career?

    1. _____

    2. _____

    3. _____

39. What are your three greatest *weaknesses* as an organization?

    1. _____

    2. _____

    3. _____

Be your own management consultant. If you were called in to your own company to report to management areas of weakness, what would you immediately think of? Sometimes, just strengthening your business in one area can change the results that your business is getting overnight.

40. What are your three biggest *obstacles* to achieving higher levels of sales and profitability?

    1. _____

    2. _____

    3. _____

If your goal is to increase your sales and profitability, why aren't they higher already? What is holding you back? What is standing in the way?

41. What are the three greatest potential *threats* to your business today? What are the worst things that could go wrong in the short term?

    1. _____

    2. _____

    3. _____

What steps could you take to make sure that they didn't happen, or that you could respond effectively if they did?

42. Looking into the future, what are the three *worst things* that could happen to hurt your business one year from today?

    1. _____

    2. _____

    3. _____

Even if there is only a 5 percent chance of something major happening that could threaten the health of your business, write it down and develop a fallback plan if it should occur.

43. What three steps could you take immediately to *guard against* these possible dangers to the health and survival of your company?

    1. _____

    2. _____

    3. _____

Never trust to luck or assume that everything is going to be all right. Hope is not a strategy.

44. What are the three areas of *greatest opportunity* for the future, based on the trends in your business?

    1. _____

    2. _____

    3. _____

Fully 80 percent of products and services in common usage five years from today will be new or different. The more you look forward and think about the opportunities of tomorrow, the more opportunities you will discover.

45. What three steps could you take immediately to *take advantage* of these opportunities?

    1. _____

    2. _____

    3. _____

Begin today to allocate time, money, people, and resources to developing the products and services of tomorrow.

46. What three *core competencies* or skills should you begin developing today to ensure that you will be ready for the opportunities of tomorrow?

    1. _____

    2. _____

    3. _____

Each business is started and built around certain core competencies. To succeed with the products and services of tomorrow, you will need to develop the new core competencies that will be required at that time. Since developing these competencies takes time, begin today.

47. What are you doing today in your business that you would *avoid* if you had to do it over, knowing what you now know?

    1. _____

    2. _____

    3. _____

It is estimated that fully 70 percent of your decisions will turn out, in the fullness of time, to be wrong. Be prepared to cut your losses if you conclude that you wouldn't get into something again today if you had it to do over.

48. What *organizational changes* should you make in your business, with regard to people, activities, work flow, and expenses, to improve both effectiveness and efficiency?

    1. _____

2. _____

3. _____

Be prepared to reorganize continually, whenever you get new information or the market changes unexpectedly.

49. How could you *restructure* to shift more of your time and resources into the top 20 percent of activities that account for 80 percent of your profits?

    1. _____

    2. _____

    3. _____

Whatever changes you would make to ensure survival sometime in the future, do them now. Focus on cash flow, on sales and revenue generation, and the most profitable use of your time and resources.

50. Imagine that your business burned to the ground today. What products, services, and activities would you *start up again* immediately? Which customers would you immediately target for acquisition?

    1. _____

    2. _____

    3. _____

51. What products, services, or activities would you *not start up again* today if your business burned

to the ground? Which customers would you not try to acquire?

1. _____

2. _____

3. _____

Be prepared to reinvent yourself and your business every six months. The rule is simple: Change before you have to!

52. Analyze every step of your business activities. What could you *simplify, outsource, eliminate, or discontinue* altogether?

1. _____

2. _____

3. _____

Continually look for ways to reengineer to do the job faster, better, cheaper, and more simply. Always ask, "Why are we doing it this way?"

53. What could you do to simplify any business process by *reducing* the number of steps in the process?

1. _____

2. _____

3. _____

There is a direct relationship between the number of steps and the potential for additional mistakes, higher costs, and longer delays. When you deliberately reduce the number of steps, you increase speed and efficiency, and you reduce the cost of the activity.

54. What activities could you *eliminate* completely to speed up the process of producing your products and services?

    1. _____

    2. _____

    3. _____

Many activities slip into the work process and remain there, gumming up the works for no good reason. Look for activities that you could eliminate without loss of efficiency.

55. What activities could you *outsource* to other individuals or companies to free yourself to sell and deliver more of your products?

    1. _____

    2. _____

    3. _____

Any product or service that is not essential to the generation of sales and revenues is a candidate for outsourcing. Companies that specialize in these services can almost always do them better, faster, and cheaper than you can do them internally.

56. What activities could you *discontinue* altogether without substantial loss of sales or revenue?

    1. _____

2. _____

3. _____

Imagine that you, a turnaround specialist, are called in to take a hard look at every activity. Which activities would you tell the management to discontinue, especially if the survival of the business was at stake?

57. Is there any *person* in your business life—a customer, employee, associate—who, knowing what you now know, you wouldn't hire, take on, or get involved with today?

1. _____

2. _____

3. _____

Fully two-thirds of people don't work out over time. They either do a mediocre job or a bad job. Only keep the people you would hire back if they applied for their jobs again today.

58. If you could start your business or career over again today, what would you do *differently?*

1. _____

2. _____

3. _____

What would you do more of? Less of? Start? Stop altogether? What advice would you give to someone else contemplating going to work in your field?

59. What skills, abilities, talents do you have that have been most responsible for your *successes* to date?

    1. _____

    2. _____

    3. _____

Each person has special abilities that make them different from anyone else. What are yours? What have you done in the past that has earned you the most praise and accomplishments? What do you enjoy doing more than anything else?

60. If you could be *excellent* at anything, what skills or abilities would be most helpful to you in achieving your most important goals?

    1. _____

    2. _____

    3. _____

Imagine that you could wave a magic wand and suddenly become extremely good at one particular skill. Which one would you choose?

61. What *actions* are you going to take immediately as a result of your answers to the above questions?

    1. _____

    2. _____

    3. _____

Leadership is not position. It is action. The purpose of all planning and analysis is action—now. Action orientation is a hallmark of leaders and top people in every field.

As Einstein said, "Nothing happens until something moves." In what way are you going to move differently from this day forward?

CHAPTER TEN

Simplify Your Life

"Treat people as if they were what they ought to be and you help them become what they are capable of being."

—JOHANN WOLFGANG VON GOETHE

Everyone has too much to do and too little time today. You feel overwhelmed with your duties, tasks, and responsibilities. As a leader, those duties, tasks, and responsibilities are multiplied. The challenge is for you to simplify your life in such a way that you spend more time doing the things that are most important to you and less time doing those things that are not at all important. A great leader is someone who is effective, positive, in control, generally content, and even-keeled. If you are overwhelmed, you are probably none of these things. Simplifying your life will not only make you a happier person, it will significantly increase your success as a leader.

In this final chapter, you will learn a variety of methods, techniques, and strategies that you can use to reorganize and restructure your life, simplify your activities, get more done, and enjoy more personal time and time with your family than ever before. Let's begin.

Determine Your True Values

The starting point for simplifying your life is for you to decide exactly what is most important to you. What are your values? What are your core beliefs? What do you care about more than anything else?

The most important question that you must ask, and answer, throughout your life is, "What do I really want to do with my life?" What you want to do with your life will invariably be an expression of your *irreducible essence*, the person that you truly are, deep inside.

To simplify your life, you should set peace of mind as your highest goal, and then organize your life around it. Whatever brings you peace, satisfaction, joy, and the feeling of value and importance is *right* for you. Whatever causes you stress, distraction, unhappiness, or irritation is *wrong* for you. You must have the courage to organize your life so you are doing more and more of the things that give you the greatest joy and satisfaction and less and less of the things that take away from your joy and satisfaction.

Decide Exactly What You Want

In every study I have ever seen and in every interview I've had with unhappy people, I have found that they have one thing in common: no clear goals. They have a lot of wishes, hopes, and desires, but they do not have goals to which they are committed. As a result, their lives go around in circles, leaving them feeling dissatisfied and empty most of the time.

Start deciding what you want by writing out a list of at least 10 goals that you would like to accomplish in the next year. After you have written out this list, review the 10 goals and then ask this question: "What one goal, if I achieved it in the next 24 hours, would have the greatest positive impact on my life?"

Select Your Major Definite Purpose

This goal usually leaps out at you from the page. It is the one thing that would have the greatest positive impact on your life. Whatever it is, put a circle around it. You are now ready to reorganize your life and simplify your activities.

Your most important goal becomes your *major definite purpose*. Then make a list of everything you can think of that you can do to achieve that goal. Organize the list by priority, by what is more important and what is less important. Then immediately begin the most important thing that you identified to achieve your most important goal.

Throughout the day, think about your goal. When you get up in the morning, think about your goal. When you go to bed at night, think about your goal. Do something every day that moves you toward the achievement of the most important goal you have. This action alone will simplify and streamline your life in ways that you cannot imagine.

Get Your Life in Balance

The key to balance is to be sure that your exterior activities are congruent, and in alignment, with your interior values. A sense of happiness, peace, joy, and relief comes when you return to your values and make sure that everything you do is consistent with them.

On the other hand, most of your stress, unhappiness, negativity, and dissatisfaction comes from attempting to do things in the outer world that are in conflict with your most important inner values.

Use the 20/10 exercise. Imagine that you have $20 million, cash, in the bank, tax-free. Imagine that you also only have 10 years to live, spend, and enjoy the $20 million. What changes would you make in your life?

One of the most important keys to simplification is to imagine no limitations on anything you would want to be or have or do. Imagine that you have all the time and money you need. Imagine that you have all the skills and abilities that you need. Imagine that you have all the friends and contacts. Imagine that you could do anything that you wanted. What would it be?

Practice Zero-Based Thinking

As we have discussed before, in zero-based thinking you draw a line under every past decision or commitment. Then ask the question, "Knowing what I now know, is there anything that I am doing today that I would not do again if I had to do it over?"

This is an extremely liberating question. Fully 70 percent of everything you do will turn out to be wrong in the fullness of time. To simplify your life, you must be willing to admit, on a go-forward basis, that you are not *perfect*.

Be prepared to say the magic words, "I was wrong!" Since you are going to be wrong much of the time, the sooner you admit it, the sooner you can simplify and improve your life.

Be willing to say, "I made a mistake." Most of the things that you do, especially in business and your career, will turn out to be mistakes in time. There is nothing wrong with this. This is how everyone learns and grows. What is wrong is to refuse to correct the mistake because our ego is invested in being "right."

Gerald Jampolski once asked, "Do you want to be right, or do you want to be happy?" You have to make this decision for yourself.

Finally, learn to regularly say, "I changed my mind." It is absolutely amazing how many people dig themselves into holes of stress, anger, frustration, and dissatisfaction because they are not willing to admit that they have changed their mind. This is not for you. You must stand back and look at your entire life. Is there anything in your life that you would not get into again today if you had to do it over? If there is, have the courage to admit that you have made a mistake (which all people do), and then take the steps to change.

There are only four ways to change the quality of your life: you can do *more* of some things, or you can do *less* of other things. You can *start* doing something that you are not doing today, or you can *stop* doing something else altogether. What is it going to be?

Reorganize Your Activities

Stand back and look at your life. Especially examine the parts of your life that are causing you stress and frustration. How could you reorganize those areas of your life so that you are doing more and more of those things that give you the greatest happiness and fewer and fewer of other things?

Reorganize your life so that you are doing more tasks of a similar nature at the same time. Start a little earlier, work a little harder, stay a little later. Do several tasks at once, rather than spreading them out.

Continually think about how you could reorganize your life to make it simpler and better.

Restructure Your Work

Remember to apply the 80/20 rule to everything you do. Eighty percent of the value of everything you do will be contained in 20 percent of the actions that you take. This means that fully 80 percent of the things you do have little or no value.

The secret to restructuring your work (and your life) is to spend more and more time doing the 20 percent of things that contribute the very most to your life and work. Simultaneously, you should spend less and less time doing those things that contribute very little. Sometimes, you should stop doing them at all.

The worst use of time is to do very well what need not be done at all.

Reengineer Your Personal Life

The whole process of reengineering is based on the exercise of reducing steps in any process. In business, we encourage people to make a list of all the steps in a particular work process. Then, we look for a way to reduce the number of steps by at least 30 percent the first time through. This is usually quite easy.

In your own life, there are three keys to reengineering your life, reducing steps, and simplifying your activities:

First, delegate everything that you possibly can to other people. The more things of low value that you delegate, the more time you free up and the more time you will have for the things that make a real difference that only you can do.

Second, outsource everything in your business that can be done by other companies that specialize in that activity. Most companies are bogged down in activities that other companies can do for them better and more efficiently, and usually at a lower price.

Third, eliminate all low value or no value activities. As Nancy Reagan said, "Just say no!" to anything that is not the highest and best use of your time.

Reinvent Yourself Regularly

Imagine that your company, your job, and your career disappeared overnight, and you had to start all over again. What would you do differently?

Imagine that you had to combine and recombine your education and experience into a new career or field of activity. What would you really love to do, if you had all the skills, ability, and money that you needed?

You should be reinventing yourself regularly, at least once each year. Stand back and look at your life and career and ask yourself, "If I was not now doing this, knowing what I now know, would I get into it?"

If the answer is "No," then your next question is, "How do I get out, and how fast?"

Set Priorities on Everything You Do

One of the best ways to simplify your life is to reorganize your life according to priorities. Realize and admit to yourself that most of the things you do have no or low value. By setting priorities, you focus more and more of your time on doing those few things that really make a difference in your life.

The most important word in setting priorities is *consequences*. If something is important, the potential consequences of doing it or not doing it are high. If something is unimportant, the potential consequences of doing it or not doing it are low.

Use the ABCDE Method to set priorities in every area of your life:

A: Tasks that are important, that have serious consequences, and that must be done or you will get into real trouble or problems

B: Tasks that you should do that have mild consequences, but that can be put off while you do your *A* tasks

C: Things that are nice to do but have no consequences. Returning a phone call to a friend or going out for lunch with a coworker are *C* tasks, with no consequences. They have no effect on your life, one way or the other.

D: Tasks that you can delegate to others, who can do them at least as well as you

E: Tasks that you can eliminate altogether because they are no longer as important as your *A* tasks

Here is the rule: Never do a *B* task when an *A* task is not done. Never do a *C* task when a *B* task is left undone. Never give into the temptation to clear up small tasks first.

When you start each working day, identify your most important task, your *A-1* task. Whatever it is, start to work on that, and stay on that until it is complete. This will simplify your life enormously.

Ask yourself, every hour of every day, "What can I, and only I, do, that if done well, will make a real difference?" Whatever your answer to this question, work on that above all others.

Set Priorities on Your Life and Work

The only way that you can simplify your life and gain control over your time is by not doing certain things. You are already too busy. Your dance card is full. It is impossible to simplify your life by simply learning how to be more efficient and effective and still working on more things. Instead, you have to *stop* doing as many things as possible.

In order to begin a new task, you must stop or discontinue an old task. In order to get into something new, you must get out of something old. You are already overworked. You cannot do more than you are already doing.

Practice *creative abandonment* with those tasks and activities that are no longer as valuable and important as others. Instead, do fewer and fewer things, but do things of higher value. This is the key to simplifying your life.

Plan Your Time In Advance

Remember the saying: "Proper Prior Planning Prevents Poor Performance," often called the 6-P formula. What this actually means is that you save 90 percent of the time you need to get through the day by planning every step in advance. It is almost miraculous!

Plan your year in advance, especially vacations with your family and friends. Book them, pay for them, and take that time off your calendar, exactly as if they were appointments with your biggest and most important customer.

Plan each month in advance. Lay it out in front of you and determine how you are going to spend the time. You will be amazed at how much more productive you are, and how much simpler your life is, by the very act of planning your months in advance.

Plan every week in advance, preferably the week before. Sit down and plan every day, using the 70 percent rule, which says that you should commit no more than 70 percent of your time. Leave yourself some slack in the system so that you have time for unexpected emergencies and delays.

Plan each day in advance, preferably the night before. Make a list of everything you have to do. Organize it by priority. Identify your *A*-1 task, and be ready to begin on that task first thing in the morning.

Delegate Everything Possible

When you start your career, you have to do everything yourself. But if you are going to grow, evolve, and become highly effective and well paid, you must delegate everything possible to anyone else who can possibly do the task.

Use your hourly rate as a measure. How much do you earn per hour? (If you earn $50,000 per year, your hourly rate is $25 per hour.)

Delegate everything to anyone who can do the task at a lower hourly rate than you want to make. It is sometimes better for you to sit and simply think, using your creative powers, than it is for you to do low-paying tasks that tire you out and consume your time.

When you delegate to other people, make sure that they have the proven ability to do it. Delegation is not abdication. Once you have delegated a task, you must supervise it and regulate it to make sure that it is done on time, on schedule, and on budget.

Focus on Higher-Value Tasks

Keep organizing and reorganizing your work so that you are spending more and more time on those few tasks that have the highest possible value. The most important time management question, which you ask and answer every hour of every day, is, "What is the most *valuable use* of my time right now?"

Whatever your answer to that question, be sure that you are working on that every minute of every day.

Focus on Every Job

This is one of the greatest ways to simplify your life. Select your most important task, your *A*-1; start on that task, and then discipline yourself to work on it single-mindedly until it is complete. Time management experts have found that if you start and stop a task several times, you can increase the amount of time necessary to complete that task by as much as 500 percent.

On the other hand, when you remain focused on a task, you can reduce the amount of time necessary to complete a task by 80 percent. This gives you a 400 percent return on the investment of your time and energy on a task. All that extra time then becomes available to you to do other things in your life that give you more joy and satisfaction.

Reduce Your Paperwork

Use the TRAF method to reduce your paperwork and get through large quantities of newspapers and magazines.

T = Toss. These are the things that you throw away immediately without reading them. This habit alone is a great time saver and simplifier.

R = Refer. These are things that you refer to other people to handle, rather than bothering with them yourself.

A = Action. These are the things that you personally need to take action on. Put these into a red file; this is what you work on, organized by priority, throughout the day.

F = File. These are the things that have to be filed for later. But remember two things. Fully 80 percent of the things you file are never referred to again. And second, whenever you order something to be filed, you create work and complicate someone else's life. Don't do this unless it is absolutely essential.

Choose Quiet

Develop the habit of leaving your radio off when you travel, especially with your family and friends. When you come home at night, leave the television off. Whenever you leave radios and televisions off, you create a "sound vacuum" that attracts communication, interaction, and the true joys of family and personal life.

Use a TIVO system to record the programs that you like, without commercials, so that you can watch them when you want, at your own convenience.

When you get up in the morning, resist the temptation to turn on the television. Instead, spend a few minutes reading something educational, motivational, or inspirational. Take some time to plan your day. Take some time to think about who you are and what you want, rather than filling your mind with the noise of endless television or radio.

Put Your Relationships First

Remember, most of the enjoyment and satisfaction you get in life will come from your interactions with other people. Put the most important people in your life at the top of your list of priorities. Put everything else below them.

Imagine that you only had six months left to live. What would you do? How would you spend your time, if you only had six months left?

Whatever your answer to this, I'm sure it does not involve earning more money or getting back to the office to return phone calls!

How would you change your life if you won a million dollars cash in the lottery tomorrow, tax free? Think about how you would change your life if you had all the money that you wanted or needed. In almost every case, you would imagine the things that you would want to do with the people that you care about the most.

Don't wait until you win a million dollars or have only six months to live before you start to spend more and more time with the most important people in your life.

Take Excellent Care of Your Physical Health

You can simplify your life by eating less and eating better.

You can simplify your life by exercising regularly and getting thinner.

You can simplify your life by getting regular medical and dental check-ups.

You can simplify your life by eating proper nutrients and taking excellent care of yourself.

Imagine that you had saved your money all your life and had finally bought a million-dollar racehorse. How would you *feed* that horse? I can promise you that you would not feed that horse fast food, junk food, sodas, and potato chips. You would feed that horse the finest foods you could find in the whole world.

You are 10 times—100 times—more valuable than a million-dollar racehorse. Feed yourself with the same kind of care that you would feed a multimillion-dollar horse. Take good care of your health.

Practice Solitude Daily

Take 30 to 60 minutes each day to sit in silence with yourself. Take the time to listen to yourself, and to your inner voice.

The practice of solitude will transform your life. In solitude, you will get ideas and insights that will change everything you do.

When you practice solitude on a regular basis, you will feel a strong sense of calm, quiet, creativity, and relaxation. You will emerge from your periods of solitude feeling wonderful about yourself and your life.

Solitude is one of the most wonderful joys available to the human being. And it costs nothing except the discipline to sit quietly for 30 to 60 minutes by yourself on a regular basis. Give it a try.

Summary

Simplify your life by practicing the preceding ideas over and over, until they become automatic and easy. Make it a habit to look for ways to do fewer things but more important things. Make it a habit to simplify your life and simultaneously increase the joy and satisfaction that you receive. Go for it!

Index

Friendship Factor, 95
frugality, 79, 99
future, focus on, 28–29

genius, qualities of, 160–161
Giuliani, Rudy, 24
goals
    of communication, 179–180
    as creativity triggers, 164
    determining personal, 226–227
    in developing vision, 17
    focus on future, 28–29
    in problem solving, 162
    self-awareness and, 36, 50
    setting and achieving, 5, 55, 108
    in setting objectives, 56–57
    shared goals of teams, 147–148
Goethe, Johann Wolfgang von, 28, 225
Golden Rule Management, 95
Goldsmith, Marshall, 7, 155
Goleman, Daniel, 183–184
Good to Great (Collins), 95–96, 115
GOSPA Method, 56–62
Green, Robert, 19
Green Bay Packers, 4

Hamel, Gary, 16
Harvard University, predictions for 1952, 3–4
Hawthorne principle, 96, 103
Henderson, Bruce, 6
high consideration factor, 153–154
higher-value tasks, 234–235
hiring bonuses, 121
Hitler, Adolf, 19–20
honesty, 21–23, 30, 182
humility, 23–25, 30, 169
Huntsman, Jon, 21

improvement, customer desire for, 196–197
independence needs, of employees, 134, 139
innovation, 5–6, 78, 99–100
    business success and, 104–105
    customer focus in, 103
    sources of, 105
integrity, 21–23, 30, 182
Intel, 78
intelligence principle, 71–73
interdependence needs, of employees, 134–136, 139

Internet employment advertisements, 122
interviews
    employment, 122–123, 124–125
    law of three, 124–125

Jampolski, Gerald, 229
job descriptions, 120–121, 130
Johnson, Samuel, 18
Jones, Charlie, 24
Juran, Joseph, 66

Kaizan Principle, 168
Knowing What I Now Know (KWINK), 67–69, 70
knowledge workers, 107, 159–160
KWINK (Knowing What I Now Know) principle, 67–69, 70

ladder analogy, 57–58
law of cause and effect, 81–82, 162
law of concentration, 101
law of the excluded alternative, 6
law of three, 124–125
Laws of Power, The (Green), 19
leadership
    character and, 14–15, 21–23, 30–31, 180
    clarity of, 149–150, 153
    Leader's Questionnaire, 195–221
    leading by example, 6–7, 28, 108, 149–150
    military principles of strategy, 53–82
    qualities of, 15–30
    responsibilities of, 5–8
    roles of manager, 85–98
    simplification process and, 225–238
Leadership (Giuliani), 24
Leader's Questionnaire, 195–221
learning process
    continuous learning, 24–25
    decision making in, 175
    mistakes in, 136–139, 150–151, 228–229
Lincoln, Abraham, 186
listening
    keys to, 187–188
    in meetings, 135–136
logos, 180
Logotherapy, 8
Lombardi, Vince, 4

Mackenzie, Alec, 56
management by exception, 91, 151–152

patience, 19–20, 95
Patton, George, 77
peace of mind, as value, 226
people-building, business success and,
  106–111
perception
  first impressions, 182–183
  persuasion and, 184–185
performance
  expectations for, 74, 89, 128–133
  feedback mechanisms, 128–131
  by leaders, 8
  in persuasion, 181
  stages of team, 151
  standards for, 93, 108, 130–131, 147–148,
  153
performing stage of teams, 151
perseverance, 19–20
personal power
  in communication process, 180–181,
  182, 191
  in persuasion, 181
persuasion
  keys to, 181–182
  motivation and, 184–185
Peters, Tom, 7
physical health, 237–238
placement agencies, 122
planning
  for accomplishing objectives, 59–60
  importance of, 233–234
  as manager role, 86–87
  managing the plan, 61–62
  market, 5–6
  measure of planning ability, 87
  scenario, 26–27, 76
  shared plans of teams, 148–149
  Six P Formula, 87, 233–234
  by sports teams, 154–155
point scoring system of decision making,
  172–173
politeness, in persuasion, 181–182
positioning, 181, 197–199
positive attitude, 28–29, 132
positive multiplier effect, 7
Prahalad, C. K., 16
praise, 128–129, 131, 186
preparation, for meetings, 183
presentation skills, 189–190
priorities, 6
  in organizing activities, 60

in personal life, 231–233
self-awareness and, 36, 50
problem solving, 6, 103, 159–170
  blocking assumptions in, 161
  conflict resolution in, 152, 155–156
  creative thinking in, 160–161, 164–168
  delegating, 174–175
  genius, qualities of, 160–161
  importance of, 159
  mistakes and, 168–169
  nature of problem, 169–170
  principle of constraints, 169–170
  systematic approach to, 160, 161–164
productivity
  in business success, 99–100
  factory model of, 92–93
  planning time in advance, 233–234
  teamwork in improving, 144
profitability, 78, 87, 101–103, 202, 211, 216
promises, keeping, 22, 209
psychographic factors, 198
purpose
  determining business, 17
  determining personal, 227

qualitative goals, 56–57
qualities, of leadership, 15–30
quality, 22
  business success and, 103–104, 211
  continuous improvement in, 6, 168
  of customer service, 81, 100–101
quantitative goals, 56–57
questions
  for business success, 63–65
  as creativity triggers, 164
  in customer service, 100–101
  in Leader's Questionnaire, 195–221
  in listening process, 188
  pointed, importance of, 36
  self-awareness, 36–50
  for setting objectives, 55–56
quiet time, 236

reading, importance of, 24–25
Reagan, Nancy, 231
reality
  facing, 70
  Reality Principle, 22
reengineering
  in business, 105–106, 217
  in personal life, 230–231

About the Author

Brian Tracy is a professional speaker, trainer, and consultant and is the chairman of Brian Tracy International, a training and consulting company based in Solana Beach, California. He is also a self-made millionaire.

Brian learned his lessons the hard way. He left high school without graduating and worked as a laborer for several years. He washed dishes, stacked lumber, dug wells, worked in factories, and stacked hay bales on farms and ranches.

In his mid-twenties, he became a salesman and began climbing up through the business world. Year by year, studying and applying every idea, method, and technique he could find, he worked his way up to become chief operating officer of a $265–million development company.

In his thirties, he enrolled at the University of Alberta and earned a bachelor of commerce degree; then he earned a masters in business administration from Andrew Jackson University. Over the years, he has worked in twenty-two different companies and industries. In 1981, he began teaching his success principles in talks and seminars around the country. Today, his books, audio programs, and video seminars have been translated into thirty-five languages and are used in fifty-two countries.

Brian has shared his ideas with more than 4 million people in forty-five countries since he began speaking professionally. He has served as a consultant and trainer for more than 1,000 corporations. He has lived and practiced every principle in this book. He has taken himself and countless thousands of other people from frustration and underachievement to prosperity and success.

Brian Tracy calls himself an "eclectic reader." He considers himself not an academic researcher but a synthesizer of information. Each year he spends hundreds of hours reading a wide variety of newspapers, magazines, books, and other materials. In addition, he listens to many hours of audio programs, attends countless seminars, and watches numerous videotapes on subjects of interest to him. Information gleaned from radio, television, and other media also adds to his knowledge base.

Brian assimilates ideas and information based on his own experience and that of others and incorporates them into his own experience. He is the bestselling author of more than forty books, including *Maxi-*

mum Achievement, Advanced Selling Strategies, Focal Point, and *The 100 Absolutely Unbreakable Laws of Business Success.* He has written and produced more than 300 audio and video learning programs that are used worldwide.

Brian is happily married and has four children. He lives on a golf course in San Diego. He travels and speaks more than 100 times each year and has business operations in seventeen countries. He is considered to be one of the foremost authorities on success and achievement in the world.

Brain Tracy
Speaker, Trainer, Seminar Leader

Brian Tracy is one of the top professional speakers in the world, addressing more than 250,000 people each year throughout the United States, Europe, Asia, and Australia.

Brian's keynote speeches, talks, and seminars are described as "inspiring, entertaining, informative, and motivational." His audiences include Fortune 500 companies and every size of business and association.

Call today for full information on booking Brian to speak at your next meeting or conference.

21st Century Thinking—How to outthink, outplan, and outstrategize your competition and get superior results in a turbulent, fast-changing business environment.
Advanced Selling Strategies—How to outthink, outperform, and outsell your competition using the most advanced strategies and tactics known to modern selling.
The Psychology of Success—How the top people think and act in every area of personal and business life. You'll learn countless practical, proven methods and strategies for peak performance.
Leadership in the New Millennium—How to apply the most powerful leadership principles ever discovered to manage, motivate, and get better results, faster than ever before.

Brian will carefully customize his talk for you and for your needs. Visit Brian Tracy International at www.briantracy.com for more information, or call 858-481-2977 today for a free promotional package.

You can also visit Brian's new *bizgrowthstrategies.com* website for information on how to increase your business's profitability.